MW00657740

HARPER SHANNON

Trumpets in the Morning

To Ken May
from the author
Harper Shannon
James 4:4-9

BROADMAN PRESS
Nashville, Tennessee

4225-29

ISBN: 0-8054-2529-2

Reissued in paper binding: 1978

Dewey Decimal classification: 253
Library of Congress catalog card number: 76-93912
Printed in the United States of America
5-At6914

To the members of
First Baptist Church, Dothan, Alabama,
for their confidence, patience, and love
without which this book could not
have been written

Preface

This book is the product of my twenty-three years plus in the ministry. It is a record for all who are interested to see of my experiences, observations and conclusions about the ministry. For good or for ill, here it is!

My underlying outlook and philosophy is apparent throughout. It may be that present and future changes in the society of the redeemed as well as the social order in the world will force me to alter some approaches, methodology, or even a few presuppositions. Nevertheless this is my "ministerial bent" thus far.

The nature of such a spiritual pilgrimage has necessitated the frequent use of the first person. This I deeply regret, but it seems to be unavoidable. I have consciously attempted *not* to gloss over my own shortcomings, although many may see only an egotistical peacock reflected in these pages. My only justification for recording so personal an account is the hope some other minister (or layman) might be strengthened and encouraged to victorious faith-optimism along the way of the common pilgrimage.

This work would never have been attempted without the strong encouragement of William S. Cannon and Joseph F.

Green of Broadman Press.

Special, unspeakable gratitude and appreciation must go to my secretary, Mrs. Agnes Fail, as well as to the other secretaries who have been directly involved in the preparation of the manuscript. These include Mrs. Gloria Vickery, Mrs. Georgette Hart, and Mrs. Ruth Brannon. I have often heard it said that if you want to get something done, give it to a busy man and he will give it to his secretary! These dear ladies, faithful co-laborers in the Lord, have shared a shocking amount of the pressures involved in meeting deadlines and publication dates. Their contribution is far more than little, and I cannot avoid the redundancy of saying it would not have been accomplished without them.

Special attention must be given to the patient endurance of my family and closest friends. Most of the material within these pages has been discussed in detail on frequent occasions with the people whom I know and trust most in this world. My profuse apologies for consistently reacting like a sponge rather than a thirst-quenching stream! I have gained far more than I have given in this reciprocal relation.

My indebtedness to many authors, preachers, and scholars will be apparent to every student of theology. I claim no originality, but do believe the material has indeed become my very own. I accept full responsibility for errors, as well as for the unwittingly omitted acknowledgments.

If the reader can hear the trumpets calling to more personalized and positive Christian commitment, then my labor will indeed not have been in vain.

Contents

I

The Thrill of the Ministry

Warren Hultgren relates an experience that is recorded in Jess Moody's book *You Can't Lose for Winning.* It was an occasion when Hultgren asked a man who had gotten out of the ministry, "What do you miss most about not being in the ministry?" He replied, "I miss the trumpets in the morning." Every minister of the gospel knows something of what he is talking about. There is a thrill, a challenge, an excitement about the gospel ministry that cannot be compared to any other profession, occupation, or calling. Indeed the ministry still strikes a spark in the hearts of many of us who are engaged in the greatest enterprise of all.

The greatest challenge in life, of course, is that of being a Christian. In my opinion the greatest *thrill* is being a minister of the gospel. There is no greater excitement or commitment. With all of its problems and heartaches, with its responsibilities and tremendous demands, *the ministry is still the greatest calling.* As has been indicated, it may be the worst profession, but it is the greatest calling! I would not trade places with the President or the governor or a king. And many of my friends in the ministry feel exactly the same way.

For more than twenty-three years now I have been preaching the gospel, but I can honestly say that it has not lost its thrill, its excitement, and its challenge. This is not to say that there are not times of discouragement, frustration, and near despair. Life is like that. There are defeats and many failures. Of course I realize more than anyone how far short I am personally of being the person and the minister God intends me to be. It would be a mistake to read this book and conclude that here is a minister who has no problems, one for whom there are no moments of despondency. Yet, I love the ministry, and if ever or whenever I lose the excitement, thrill, anticipation, and expectation now associated with the gospel ministry then I know I will get out.

I still hear the trumpets in the morning, the call to a new day, the excitement, the eagerness of being of ministry, of service, of doing God's will. There is indeed no greater thrill. I thank God for his calling me to preach. It is hearing those trumpets in the morning that often keeps me going. I pray this shared testimony might enable some discouraged fellow pilgrim to hear the unmistakable sound again.

Theme of the Book

The theme of this book is simply that *the gospel ministry is the most thrilling and dynamic experience a person can have* on this earth. It is my prayerful desire to encourage and strengthen other ministers, my fellow workers, the co-laborers in the gospel of Christ. Especially would I like to inspire and encourage the younger men, preacher boys, students, and those young people who are just now contemplating the call to the ministry. There is a lot of frustration and disillusionment in the ministry today. Many young people are challenged by everything else in the world except the gospel ministry. This book will fulfil its purpose if somehow the vision of the challenging and thrilling life can captivate the minds and hearts of the young and old alike who are susceptible to the divine call.

Many times I can recall in my own experience that there were moments that literally cried out for a word of encouragement. Thank God, on many such occasions some dear friend (often quite unconsciously) stepped into the gap with just the right word, at just the right time, and lifted me up from the slough of despair. One of the things I would like to do in heaven is be able to recall all the encouraging words spoken to me on earth, and take time to personally express gratitude to those who helped both wittingly and otherwise.

My Call to the Ministry

Actually from the time I was a very little boy I have had something of the sense of the call to preach. My conversion to Christ occurred at the early age of seven years, but I can distinctly remember a conscious desire to be a minister of the gospel before my conversion. If the advice of some were to be followed today, I would not have been baptized, nor allowed to begin my ministry until many years later! The fact is it would be quite difficult for me to ascertain in point of time the initial consciousness on my part of the divine call to the ministry. It is actually quite difficult to distinguish between a childish fancy and the beginning of a responsible and responsive understanding to God's call to preach, at least as far as the specific time is concerned. This is not to say that I was not conscious of a definite call very early in life. But the call came so very early I cannot ascertain just when it was responsibly recognized.

As a young lad I used to preach to my parents and the other members of my family. It was more than playing church. It was a conscious although somewhat childish and immature activity based upon the attitude that God wanted me to be a preacher. There was apparently no parental or outside pressure of any kind. There are no preachers in my family except myself. I seem to be the only black sheep! There was no known direct influence or pressure brought to bear by any minister or Sunday School teacher or RA leader. I have never been able to adequately explain my childish commitment to the gospel ministry apart from the implantation in a young mind and heart of a divine call. I believe that God was planting the seed that would later bring fruition and conscious response on my part at this very early age.

Of course I am greatly aware of a tremendous indebtedness here to divine providence in my being born into a Christian home with active Christian parents. If this had not been the case, then of course I would not have been converted at such an early age nor could I possibly have had a call to the ministry at such an early age. At least I could not have responded to it. I would not have understood it otherwise. It was in the context of a Christian home and family that my conversion experience was precipitated, as well as my call to the gospel ministry, although both of these must be attributed to divine grace and initiative.

Actually I can remember two basic sermons I used to preach as a lad. One was on "The End of the World." I suppose I had heard my pastor or some revival preacher preach on the final destruction of the world by fire from Peter. This captivated my childish imagination. And although I do not think that in my formal ministry I have ever preached a sermon on this subject, it was my first. I can vividly recall opening the Bible (which I could not read) and dramatically proclaiming that God would one day destroy the entire world (not part or half, but the whole world) in divine judgment for man's wickedness. As the Lord had judged the world and its wickedness in the flood recorded in the Old Testament, so the divine wrath was sure to come in the future, but this time by fire.

The second sermon, however, has continued to be a basic part of my life and ministry. It was simply entitled "Only Believe." Somehow in my childish imagination and early intellectual explorations I became captivated by that which I believe to this day to be fundamental to the gospel ministry and the Christian life, namely, faith in God which is active commitment and obedience to Jesus Christ. To believe in Jesus was the way to be saved, the proper path to living the Christian life, and the basis of assurance of a heavenly home.

Desire to Know the Bible

Some of the earliest recollections of my childhood are those of a burning desire to know more about the Bible. I can remember the visits of pastors and preacher friends to our home. How eagerly I would sit and listen to whatever they had to say to my father and/or mother as they discussed Scripture interpretations, Bible doctrines, problem passages, and favorite sermons and texts. It was a thrill; I was captivated by anyone who knew something about the Bible and I would listen as long as they would talk, sitting quietly, absorbing, wondering, wanting to ask many questions but usually lacking the courage to do so.

The last time George W. Truett spoke in Alabama he conducted a week-long crusade in the Municipal Auditorium of Birmingham. I could not have been much more than ten or eleven years old. With my pastor I attended every service. Although I had no idea at the time who this great man really was, I attended and listened intently because he was a preacher, and he was talking about God, the Bible, and the things of the Spirit. The most memorable recollections of my childhood are those of listening to a preacher of the gospel. There was nothing else quite like it for me as a lad.

My first formal sermon was preached at the age of fourteen in the Huffman Baptist Church of Birmingham. I was invited to be the Youth Week speaker. This was something new in those days, and although I had been giving devotionals and short inspirational talks for several years, this was my big opportunity. I did not shrink back but accepted it with enthusiasm. Although the pastor felt that perhaps the young lad who had consistently expressed a desire to preach would not be able to fill the time allotted on his first occasion, some of my friends remind me to this day that my first sermon was forty-two minutes long!

I shall never forget the comments of the pastor, James E. Davidson, after my first sermon. He said in my presence to my parents and other friends, "The thing that impressed me most about his message was that he was preaching to the *people*. He had something to say to those who were here. He was not preaching out the window." This man, my father in the ministry, has made indelible impressions on my life for God and for good.

As a teen-age preacher boy in high school my desire to know the Bible and to have opportunities to share my faith with others became more intense. Another pastor, James H. Butler, gave me a copy of David Smith's *Life and Letters of Paul*. It read like a novel! I shall never forget the excitement of Paul's letter to the Romans written in modern language.

It seemed to me that the thesis of this letter was the basis of the Christian faith and that it would become the very basis of my entire ministry, namely, that justification is by faith. Perhaps that is the reason my love for Paul's epistle to the capitol of the Roman Empire has increased rather than diminished to this day. It is still my favorite epistle.

One of the earliest recollections of a problem in regard to the ministry that I can recall is the occasion when I wondered how a preacher in the seminary or college classroom could make less than a hundred on an exam. It seemed to me he ought to be able to know *all* the answers! He ought to know all about the Bible. He ought to be able to explain all of the doctrines of the faith. How in the world could a man entrusted with the spiritual care of the souls of men not know all the facts about the Bible and have all the right words to say in any and all given situations!

Of course it did not take very long as a student in college and seminary to realize that the minister of the gospel does *not* have all the answers. But the sense of *responsibility* associated with being a minister of the gospel is the thing that captivated me as a young person. The eternal destinies of people were at stake. Even a medical doctor can make a mistake which results in the physical death of a human being. But this was not as serious to me as dealing with the eternal soul and the ultimate spiritual destiny of a human being. This sense of deep responsibility for the minister has remained with me unto this very day. Whatever else the ministry is, it is not something to be taken lightly.

A Professional Optimist

Frequently I have been called by my closest personal friends, "a professional optimist." This was perhaps done in a half-joking way at first because of what was believed to be my inability to accept the reality of defeat. But there is an element of tremendous truth here. Actually I developed a personal and practical philosophy of life based on positive thinking long before I ever heard of Norman Vincent Peale. It seems to me that the Christian, of all people, especially the *minister*, should major on the positive, the good, the beautiful, the worthy, the clean, and the pure in life. Of what value is it to always look at the gloomy and dark side of life? Why shouldn't the minister of Christ, who is the propagator of the greatest hope in the world, be a professional optimist and yet a realist?

It is not true that the Christian or the minister can afford the luxury of being unrealistic. He cannot. But there is enough ugliness in the world that cannot be overlooked, and there are enough pessimists to perennially point out the ugly and the dirty. It seems to me the minister, of all people, must constantly discipline himself towards a positive outlook on life. It does take discipline. One must periodically rule out negative thoughts, refuse to be surrounded by people who cultivate defeatist attitudes. If you think negatively then you will be defeated before you begin. Optimism, a positive outlook, and idealistic dreams are the order of the day for God's servants.

The Christian faith is not fatalism, but the Christian faith means a conscious determination to magnify the good, find the best in people, and perform the best service possible with the strength and power of the Spirit of Christ. This is what gives a sense of victory and exhilaration to the ministry. It would be easy to point out the failures, problems, the disillusionments, discouragements, the defeats, to the exclusion of the rewards, the thrills, the challenges, and the blessings. Both are present in every Christian's life, certainly in every minister's life. Our attitudes toward them, however, will be determined by and large by whether or not we have cultivated "a professional optimist" outlook on life. Remember the difference is not in what happens to the Christian and the non-Christian, but in the spiritual resources on which the Christian has to draw.

Not everyone will share this optimistic view of the ministry or the Christian life. Unfortunately, some of our brethren who are now ministers have apparently acquiesced to a negative spirit and a defensive attitude. They are simply biding time, occupying a job, filling a role, applying a little healing salve to wounded hearts and lives which cry out most fervently for help. This is a tragedy, but this does not deter the committed minister of the gospel from fulfilling his sense of commitment and consciously centering his life upon the will of God as he interprets the divine call. The fact that some ministers are startling examples of the opposite of Christian optimism is no rational excuse for our failure to be living epistles demonstrating Christlike optimism and victory in the midst of a troubled world!

The trumpets in the morning are still sounding! Some are not hearing but the problem is not with the notes being sent forth but the spiritual insensitivity of our hearing! If this book can contribute to the removal of the layers of spiritual wax that have separated our spiritual responsiveness from the opportunities and challenges of the ministry, then it will not have been in vain. My only apology for writing such a personal dissertation would be in the interest of helping some other fellow minister in the faith to a sense of triumph and victory and joy in his calling. Oh, my dear preacher friend, will you not sharpen your spiritual senses, tune up your spiritual hearing aid, and see if you cannot once again know the thrill, the excitement, the challenge of being God's minister to his people? In short will you listen with me and respond enthusiastically to the trumpets in the morning?

II

Ministerial Restlessness

There is a tremendous need for this kind of positive, optimistic emphasis in the ministry today. In fact it may well be that the greatest single need among ministers today is for a constructive and loving word of encouragement. There is an alarming amount of ministerial restlessness among the brethren. This restlessness manifests itself in the desire to look for greener pastures, the subtle suggestion that maybe my work is finished here.

Various factors contribute to this restlessness but even the casual observer recognizes many pastors are disillusioned, discouraged, and despondent. Some are ready to throw in the towel and some have already done so. Resignations with or without another place to go are seemingly the order of the day. Other ministers are *required* to resign, sometimes by direct congregational or official board request and sometimes by far more subtle and sophisticated means.

Surveys and Editorials

The Annuity Board of the Southern Baptist Convention has indicated repeatedly that many Southern Baptist ministers leave the ministry each year. Of course the statistics of the Annuity Board would reflect only those ministers who were participants in one of our denomination's programs for retirement or disability. There are unquestionably many others leaving the ministry also. These facts are alarming to say the least. When other denominations are decrying the shortage of ministers and when Southern Baptists are becoming increasingly aware of the difficulty in leading young people to commit their lives to church-related vocational service, it is imperative that we face the issue of ministerial restlessness with honesty and forthrightness. We can no longer glibly ignore this increasingly obvious and critical problem, and like the proverbial ostrich poke our heads into the sand pretending that it does not exist.

Editor Jack Harwell of the Georgia Baptist *Christian Index* has indicated in a survey in the state of Georgia that during one year there were 561 ministerial moves among Georgia Baptist churches. There were obviously many more such moves that were unreported or could not be verified. Out of these 561 moves a total of 125 included in the announcement of the resignation the following statement, "with his plans unannounced," or some such similar revealing phrase. This of course is nearly 20 percent of the total. This in itself indicates there is a great deal of ministerial dissatisfaction or at least congregational dissatisfaction with the ministry. It would be hard to ascertain which is worse. Both are real problems and obviously these experiences in Georgia could be multiplied throughout the Convention.

We are familiar with articles on why I resigned, why I left the ministry, resignation in protest, and such like. Editor L. H. Moore of the *Ohio Baptist News* recently commented on the abrupt termination of an eight-year pastorate as the result of calloused inconsiderateness in regard to the church's future as well as the pastor's. He quotes a denominational leader as indicating recently that half of the churches are not happy with their pastors and half the pastors are not happy with their churches. This statement may be beyond proof and it certainly is a subjective conclusion to say the least, but it points up dramatically the problem of ministerial restlessness in our denomination.

Although this problem has always existed to a certain degree, and no doubt the present-day increase in numbers of churches and pastors is reflected in an increased ministerial restlessness, nevertheless it is doubtful that there has ever been a time when as high a percentage of pastors and churches are dissatisfied with each other as now. The problem has reached the crisis point even for casual observers and otherwise basically optimistic witnesses.

Financial Stress

Unquestionably the financial situation of ministers and churches is a major contributing factor to this restlessness. It is not that preachers are preaching for money. It is simply that they must have money to live in order to preach! Many preachers are just simply not paid enough. Many churches do not exercise good stewardship in allocating the Lord's money, especially where the minister and his family are concerned. Again Editor Harwell in the *Christian Index* editorially commented on some financial facts of life which bear hard on preachers. He quotes the tearful lament of a young Georgia pastor as follows: "I feel I'm in the Lord's will to be in my present pastorate. We are making statistical and spiritual progress. We have unity and harmony but I absolutely cannot pay my bills with a wife and three children. I must have a dramatic increase in salary or I will have to move to a larger church or take a secular job. I don't think the Lord expects me to default on my debts or to let my family go hungry." Could not this appalling testimony be repeated a hundredfold in every one of our thirty-one Southern Baptist state conventions, and in other denominations as well?

In my own experience I have just heard of a dear layman friend who after being successful in business felt the call of God into full-time, church-related vocational service. He resigned his position, entered the seminary, graduated with a religious education degree and began serving as minister of education in a Southern Baptist church. It was necessary for him to resign, however, approximately a year later because his inadequate salary made it impossible to sufficiently provide for the basic needs of his family, let alone begin repayment on educational loans precipitated by his seminary training. He has returned to a secular position at a beginning salary of exactly twice his salary as minister of education. Again this example could be multiplied dozens of times over. It is not a mere isolated case.

Unfortunately the problems of ministerial restlessness cannot be automatically resolved by simple raises in salary or total income. It is not that simple, at least in many instances. Much discouragement and despondency is obvious *among the more affluent* ministers and churches as well as the underpaid. We have seen graphically illustrated in our twentieth-century society that financial and economic resources themselves alone cannot provide men with emotional security or peace of mind. Never have Americans had so much in this world's goods, and yet been so miserable generally speaking. So many of us are chagrined to discover that problems seem enhanced rather than resolved as a result of increased financial remunerations. On the one hand more money may bring more problems, and on the other hand when we are relieved of the economic pressures other problems seem often to automatically take their place.

One thing that a minister must have in order to continue in his work is encouragement. This is unquestionably one of his greatest needs. No human being is capable of indefinitely continuing his work against seemingly insurmountable odds without some kind of encouragement, or the feeling of accomplishment. This is especially true of the minister of the gospel, although the opposite is obviously often believed by many in our congregations. We simply cannot go on if we do not feel that we are doing some good.

It is true that many ministers cannot concentrate on the main things because of financial worries, and this ought not to be. But it is also true that the ministers whose income is substantial enough to provide for the necessities of life for them and their families must have in addition to economic security some sense of accomplishment and victory in their work. The average minister of today has some exceedingly deep personal problems and anxieties just like many of his parishioners. And he simply cannot adequately cope with them apart from some sense of accomplishment in his work.

Steps in Ministerial Decline

The secular press delights in reporting the instances of ministerial restlessness which result in moral lapses, and particularly those which result in some criminal act. It is usually front-page news when a man of the cloth absconds with the offerings or elopes with the organist or deacon's wife. But these moral lapses are occasions for grief and investigation into some basic causes. It seems to me that the optimistic and realistic consideration of the pastor and the ministry which is a part of my basic philosophy of life could be a contributing factor to stability in Christian living as well as permanence in pastor-church relationships.

Recently while traveling on a plane I had the opportunity of discussing with a lay-preacher friend the problem of ministerial moral decline. My friend indicated some rare insights into the progressively downward steps most ministers would probably follow in moving from the citadel of divine responsibility and opportunity as a minister of the gospel to a low level of immorality and personal sin. My friend analyzed these steps as follows:

(1) *Wasting of time.* Many of us ministers speak constantly of how much we have to do, how busy we are, how little time there is to get things done. But it should be obvious that we can become so busy that eventually we do nothing! Constant references to many activities can be a genuine reaction to the impossible responsibilities thrust upon one man in the limitations of time. But it also can be a defense mechanism to rationalize or excuse our indolence, or lack of self-discipline. If a minister becomes guilty of laziness and wasting time, the most efficient way to cover up for it is to be constantly talking about how busy he is in order to camouflage the issue.

(2) *Treating the sacred lightly.* This step in ministerial decline might take many forms but the more obvious would be succumbing to questionable jokes and stories both in listening and relating. Or it could demonstrate itself in too much time spent delving into the ash cans and cesspools of modern popular literature. It sometimes rears its ugly head through personal preoccupation with the promiscuous acts

of many moderns, whose practical outlook on life amounts to little more than a playboy philosophy.

Sacred things can also be treated in a flippant way by adopting a superior, liberal attitude reflected in sneers, snobbishness, and the misuse of irony and satire to deprecate the doctrinal position of someone considered to be less educated. One way to answer an argument which cannot be rationally refuted is to ridicule both the idea and the person propagating it. Another form of this is defamation of character of those who are getting the job done. If you cannot equal the other man's record then destroy his reputation so the record will not count. Too many of us have already betrayed our highest responsibility to each other by succumbing to this type of temptation.

(3) *An overevaluation of one's work.* It is very easy for the minister to convince himself that he is not paid enough (which he probably isn't). It is but one step further for him to attempt to make up for this financial lag with outside interests and enterprises. Many ministers have found it but a short step from preoccupation with outside interests for additional financial income to the condition of complete disinterest in the real challenge and opportunity of the ministry.

A minister can thus rather easily justify his interest in real estate, stocks and bonds, various sales techniques for numerous items including books, records, pictures, and so forth. He can become a tour conductor, a guide, a professional sportsman, or almost anything he sets his mind to. The problem is not so much the outside activity as it is the valuation in practical reality placed on such activity, such as the time consumed, energy expended, interest given.

(4) Finally then comes *the lust of the flesh.* Usually a man does not fall from the top to the bottom all at once. His

descent is usually much more gradual. If a man begins to waste his time, treat the sacred lightly, and focus his attention upon an overevaluation of his own personal worth, he is immediately susceptible to the sins of the flesh in an unprecedented way. Most ministers who have had moral lapses have done so only long after they have already lost the thrill of the ministry and can no longer hear the trumpets in the morning. The road downward is most frequently a slow descent rather than a sharp jump over the cliff.

Of course this is not necessarily true. Any of us is susceptible to temptation at any time. We are capable of falling to the lowest rung in a moment of weakness. Only through the persistent attitude depicted by Joseph in Egypt when he fled from Potiphar's wife can the minister assure himself of his moral strength in a moment of temptation. "Wherefore let him that thinketh he standeth take heed lest he fall" (1 Cor. 10:12).

The trumpets in the morning can not only be a call to a new day and a new opportunity but they can also call us to a consistent life of moral purity and spiritual triumph. It is not true that all ministerial restlessness is the result of moral lapse. But tragically it is certainly true that insecurity in our calling throws open the doors of temptation to an alarming degree. It is much easier for the dissatisfied minister to succumb to moral decline than for one who persists daily in pursuit of what he sincerely believes to be the greatest challenge in the world!

III

Biblical Bases for Confidence and Assurance

It may sound old-fashioned, outdated, and anything but erudite and professional, but the key to ministerial stability and strength lies in the rediscovery of familiar biblical truths for living a Spirit-directed and Spirit-infilled life. A return to authentic New Testament Christianity, especially in regard to personal, holy, victorious living, is imperative in the light of present-day circumstances. The only hope for modern ministers in the face of the adversities, responsibilities, and pitfalls of this day is to renew our personal relationship to Jesus Christ, and rediscover the practical application of fundamental biblical doctrines concerning victorious Christian living. A return to biblically-based, Christ-centered, everyday godly living is the necessity of the hour!

First, a Willing Mind

In 2 Corinthians 8:12 Paul said, "If there be first a willing mind, it is accepted according to that a man hath, and not according to that he hath not." This verse is found in the context of instructions concerning the stewardship of material possessions, but the principle readily lends itself to much broader application. In 1 Corinthians 15:58 Paul says that we should know that our labor is not in vain in the Lord. It seems to me that this is a basic assumption essential to a successful ministry. Whatever we do for God is not lost, no matter what the visible outcome—if we are serving him willingly to the best of our ability and opportunity. Success, of course, does not mean success according to human standards such as statistical records, or other visible evidences. The only criterion for adequately judging the success of our work is the knowledge that we have done the will of God.

Ministers often complain about denominational pressure and the outside goal-setting standards being thrust upon us. The truth of the matter, I am convinced, is that most of the pressure to achieve specific records is thrust upon us by ourselves! We simply do not want to be categorized as failures. We want to achieve; we want to set a good record. It is a part of human nature, but the thing that we must constantly be reminded of as ministers of the gospel is that it is not public opinion or statistical reports that constitute a successful ministry. *It is doing the best we can with the help of God and living daily in the center of his will!* If there is first a willing mind we can have the confidence that God is not demanding from us anything which we cannot produce. What a tremendous relief to know that God is reasonable!

God's Cure for Anxiety

My practical philosophy of life has been built through the years primarily on one passage of Scripture—Philippians 4:4-9. Contained within this brief passage are the basic ingredients for any minister or Christian hearing trumpets of opportunity, victory, and blessing in the morning. "Rejoice in the Lord alway: and again I say, Rejoice. Let your moderation be known unto all men. The Lord is at hand. Be careful for nothing; but in every thing by prayer and supplication with thanksgiving let your requests be made known unto God. And the peace of God, which passeth all understanding, shall keep your hearts and minds through Christ Jesus. Finally, brethren, whatsoever things are true, whatsoever things are honest, whatsoever things are just, whatsoever things are pure, whatsoever things are lovely, whatsoever things are of good report; if there be any virtue, and if there be any praise, think on these things. Those things, which ye have both learned, and received, and heard, and seen in me, do: and the God of peace shall be with you."

In my own personal life I have found quite frequently the secret to adjustment to seemingly insurmountable problems in the application of three basic principles which were discovered long ago in this passage. Paul wrote that we ought to be happy in the Lord at all times and he wrote this from a prison cell. If a Christian ever had the right to be discouraged it certainly should be while in prison! Yet Paul said that we ought to be anxious for nothing. This means that perennial worry and mental anxiety that leads to physical exhaustion, as well as spiritual defeat, is a sin. It should be avoided like the plague. Of course to give such advice is almost like the physician's advice to the woman who had a problem of worry. "If you do not quit worrying, you are going to worry yourself to death!" Obviously she then had something really to worry about.

The three principles discovered in Philippians 4:4-9 are *right praying,* verses 6 and 7; *right thinking,* verse 8; and *right acting,* verse 9.

First of all, Paul says that prayer should be made in and

about everything and it should be coupled with thanksgiving as we make our petitions known face to face with God. Prayer must be preceded by and coupled with sincere gratitude and personal thanksgivings. One reason why our prayers are often unanswered may be because of our failure to approach God with a grateful heart. There is nothing too small or insignificant to pray about. A man once reacted to my assertions about prayer with complete disbelief by saying, "You wouldn't ask God for a pair of shoes, would you?" My answer was that I would ask God unhesitatingly for a pair of shoes *if I needed* a pair of shoes and did not have any other apparent means of securing them.

The trouble with us preachers and many Christians is that we do not think God is concerned enough with the things that concern us! When discouragement comes, when problems arise, and temptation presents itself, why in the world do we not learn to take literally what Paul says, what the Bible teaches, and simply take it to the Lord in prayer? I think this is what Paul meant when he said, "Pray without ceasing." He obviously did not mean that we can stay on our knees all day in a particular posture of prayer. Rather he meant that prayer is an attitude, a communion with God. In a moment of crisis it should be the most natural thing possible for the child of God to simply "take your burden to the Lord and leave it there."

Of course this kind of frequent praying must be coupled with thanksgiving, literally centered in gratitude, which automatically leads to spiritual peace. Victory for tomorrow's temptations is to a great degree dependent upon our remembering with thanksgiving the victories of yesterday. The biblical policy is that if we pray right, the peace of God will garrison like an army around our hearts and minds literally keeping out thoughts of fear, defeat, negativism, and doubt. The word translated "keep" is a military term and is best expressed in "garrison like an army."

The peace of God is something that *passes* all human understanding. The trouble with us is that we want to find the peace that men understand, that the world can recognize, the peace that is built upon success, good records, outstanding achievements, and favorable press releases. The kind of peace that God's Word promises is the peace that is *beyond* human understanding. It is the kind of peace that the minister of the gospel has when he has had a bad year physically, the Sunday School attendance is declining, the baptismal record is at an all-time low, the budget is not being met, and the deacons are demanding production or resignation. The man of God who can maintain spiritual peace and a sense of accomplishment in the midst of such circumstances indeed has a peace that cannot be interpreted, understood, or grasped by human standards!

Of course the source of such peace is God himself. One cannot know or experience this peace of God until he has experienced peace *with* God through personal faith in Jesus Christ. There is a difference in man-made inner peace and the sweet peace which is the gift of God's grace, following a genuine experience of conversion which brings peace with God through our Lord Jesus Christ.

The second suggestion Paul makes in Philippians 4 is that of *positive thinking*. He suggests what Norman Vincent Peale has popularized in our day—we ought to magnify positive thoughts. We ought to think on things that are true, honest, just, beautiful, lovely, of good report, virtuous, and praiseworthy. The Bible says that as a man thinketh in his heart so is he. How can a minister of the gospel maintain a positive outlook towards his ministry and on life as a whole if he constantly fills his mind and soul with the negative, the ugly, the dirty, and the vile? Jesus said, "Blessed are the pure in heart: for they shall see God." If we magnify that which is pure and that which is good, we shall eventually become in attitude and practice like that which occupies both our conscious and subconscious thoughts. To a real degree we are what we think.

This principle has been illustrated in the business world in frequent cases. A salesman who does not believe in his product cannot be a success. No man can sell life insurance who has not already insured his own life. No Christian can be an effective witness for Christ who does not know Jesus Christ in a personal relationship. And no minister of the gospel can hear trumpets of victory ringing in his ears if he has already convinced himself that he cannot succeed, that he is a failure, that his day of opportunity has passed.

It is amazing how the power of suggestion can influence our behavior patterns. If a person perennially succumbs to the habit and attitude of negative, defeatist thoughts and actions, then almost inevitably and rather mechanically he will become the despondent failure he has conditioned himself to be. Although it is quite apparent that *thinking* success is not alone sufficient for victory, nevertheless few victories are accomplished without this prerequisite confidence. In short there is indeed power in positive thinking!

Paul's third suggestion is *right activity*. "Those things, which ye have both learned, and received, and heard, and seen in me, *do:* and the God of peace shall be with you" (Phil. 4:9). Much of our frustration comes from the inability to get things done. We can be so enamored with various responsibilities in the daily schedule that we do not get *anything* done. Yet one of the most therapeutic activities possible for a busy minister is to simply plunge into a desk of work, a schedule of appointments, or other responsibilities with vigor and enthusiasm. It may be that when the day is over everything has not been accomplished that should have been, but there is nothing quite as invigorating as knowing that for the past ten or twelve hours you have given yourself without reservation to the task at hand!

The example of the apostle in regard to accomplished tasks was indeed one we would do well to imitate. Paul did not hesitate to suggest to the Philippians that they emulate him in this regard. They had heard him both teach and demonstrate in daily living the principles now reiterated to them. Ignorance is no excuse, but they were not ignorant! They had both received and learned from Paul. Now it remained to put into positive action what was known.

Paul discovered the secret to victorious living. We must cultivate an attitude of perennial prayer presenting our petitions face to face before God. We must guard against negativism and defeatism by majoring on the positive and the good. But all of this will be to no avail unless having trained and disciplined our minds for positive thoughts we now transfer our energies into positive activities! The only way to quit worrying about the letters that need to be written, for instance, is to *write the letters.* The only way to quit worrying about the many things that need to be done is to *begin to do them.* There is a cathartic effect which purges our minds and hearts from negative thoughts of discouragement and despair in simply applying ourselves to the task of getting the job done!

A Good Servant of Jesus Christ

O. T. Binkley has indicated in a series of Bible lessons at Ridgecrest that in 2 Corinthians Paul enumerates several characteristics of a good servant of Jesus Christ. They are:

(1) *A sense of mission,* 1:1, 21
(2) *Competency for the task,* 2:16; 3:5
(3) *Personal integrity,* 1:17-19
(4) *A participant in the ministry of reconciliation,* 5:17-21
(5) *Possessing stamina and heart,* 4:1, 16

It ought to be obvious that a good minister of Jesus Christ should demonstrate these traits. He certainly should have a sense of mission and purpose. Aimlessness can only lead to defeat and frustration. There is no substitute for competency and efficiency. Personal integrity will be considered at length in the closing chapter of this book. Reconciliation is what the ministry is all about. Heart and stamina are essential prerequisites for any worthwhile task, especially the gospel ministry.

There is much for the modern minister to receive in the way of encouragement from an intensive and detailed study of the things that encouraged and strengthened New Testament Christians. They had problems, they had discouragements, they faced the same basic situations that we do. Only *the circumstances* have changed. Surely we can rediscover in their secrets of triumphant daily living the key that will open the door for victory in our own lives. The call goes out for a renewed emphasis on basic biblical studies from the standpoint of content as well as the inferences.

Modern ministers need to remember that true Christian service is not based upon activity but *commitment.* It is not enough just to keep busy all the time. Any minister can work long hours, stay in the office way into the night, or spend infinite days in visitation among church members and in various social activities. But *Christian service cannot be adequately measured by the extent of our activities,* number of meetings, how many committees we are members of, number of church functions, or statistical reports on visits made.

To be committed to the lordship of Jesus Christ means that the main decision has already been made. Service must be an outgrowth and an overflow of this inner commitment. Many times our searching for the will of God is in reality a seeking for a rationalization for not doing what we already know to be God's will. The outstanding need of the moment for modern-day preachers is to *get back where we started* in the ministry. Most of us in that first sermon, in our first pastorate, in the first funeral or wedding, or the first pastoral call were probably more committed in prayer to God and to positive thinking and doing the right thing than we have ever been since! God help us to get back to the simple fundamentals of the Christian faith and build on these biblical bases, confidence, and assurance commensurate with the needs of our day!

IV

The Temerity of Preaching

The title of this chapter may seem rather foreboding, so perhaps a definition of terms at the very outset will prove helpful. The dictionary definition of temerity is unreasonable contempt of danger, rashness. Synonyms for this little-used word are audacity, effrontery, nerve, and gall.

These are all aspects of the tremendous experience of preaching. Preaching certainly involves a great amount of nerve, and some would say, presumption. The apostle Paul spoke of the foolishness of the preaching. He was concerned of course primarily with the message or *kerygma,* the basic proclamation of what God had done for man in Jesus Christ. We are concerned here with the *act,* the *circumstance,* as well as the result of the preaching event. We are concerned primarily with the motive and attitude of the proclaimer and his congregation, including the basic presuppositions upon which such a situation as preaching and worship is built. The basic premise of this chapter is that preaching is an audacious act of temerity!

What is involved in this action? Is such boldness truly justified? Why should any man have the gall to attempt what the preacher does?

Presumptuous and Audacious

It was Gene E. Bartlett in his Lyman Beecher Lectures entitled *The Audacity of Preaching* published by Harper and Brothers, who first precipitated my thinking in regard to the audacity and raw nerve involved in the preaching event. I must readily acknowledge my tremendous indebtedness to him throughout the material appearing in this chapter, although I am happy to confess that these ideas have in reality become experientially my very own. Preaching, of all the claims that man can make, perhaps is the most presumptuous or at least the most audacious claim of all. The preacher affirms that man can know God in a personal relationship. He assumes that man can know who God is, and that he (man) can become a righteous and mature individual in fellowship with God. The preacher in effect claims to know the will and the Word of God and to have the ability to proclaim it. This, of course, is obviously a stupendous claim.

Who in the world is the preacher anyway? Who is this man who claims to have a relevant message from God, who dares command the attention of his congregation week after week with a "Thus saith the Lord"? He is simply one who has experienced this great event of salvation or a personal relationship with God and ventures to share his faith and experience with others. He is a sinner saved by grace just like those in his congregation. The preacher is one who has sought to know God's will and way, believes he has found it, and now wishes to share it with fellow searchers. He is one who strives to be nonegotistical, yet who realizes that the validity of his claim is obvious only as he relates his own personal experience.

The most basic needs universally of mankind in any age are those needs which have reference to sin, guilt, and redemption. Circumstances may and do change but man is basically a spiritual being created for fellowship with God who is Spirit. The gospel *is* relevant, but it must always be applied, and the application must be colloquially practical. Yet despite the constant need for interpretation of the gospel message in the light of changing circumstances in every generation, man's basic need is still spiritual. The preacher is concerned first and foremost with speaking to this particularly. All the rest will fall into proper perspective only after priority has been given to man's spiritual need for a right relationship and continuing fellowship with God.

Hindrances to Preaching

Unfortunately, there are many barriers in the way of the preacher making clear his revelation from God. Bartlett has referred to this as the secular barrier, by which he means the typical Sunday morning worship experience, very ordinary and very earthbound. People's minds are occupied with everything short of divine self-manifestation. A man's mind is occupied with his business problems. A woman's thoughts are whether or not she turned off the roast for Sunday's dinner. The attractive young lady is wistfully hoping that her choice young man will ask her to the party on Friday night. The young man who pictures himself as a modern Don Juan is whisperingly relating his conquests of the night before to his awestruck friends.

It is in this setting the brash preacher stands in the pulpit and audaciously attempts to present a message from God! Listen to Bartlett's description of this particular circumstance:

So we must come to terms with the actual hour of preaching. What a familiar scene! The people gather at the appointed time, according to their custom. Though, in theory, they reserve this hour for eternal affairs, actually they bring the world with them in a diversity of gifts and needs. Some are weary and some are angry. Some have come because it is their habit. Others know a strange compulsion. There are the seeking, the complacent, the hungry, the anxious, the discouraged. There are also those who come that particular day with a sense that they are keeping an appointment of soul; a strange readiness is about them, the whole issue of life seems to hang in so close a balance that a persuasive word can make the difference.

The service proceeds along a traditional way, for some a rich and ancient liturgy, for others a simple ordering of the elements of divine worship, for some a kind of comfortable disorder, a formalized informality. For all there will be music, prayers, and the reading of ancient, cherished words. Then for most the moment comes, that tremendous moment, when a man must stand up to preach. As his words begin, they often seem, especially to the casual onlooker, very ordinary and earthbound. There are no opening skies. There is no angel visitant. Often it seems but another vain repetition. In short, by every external evidence, it is a very ordinary occasion.

The recalling of such a time brings a haunting question: Is the Word, the very Word of God, to be heard in so prosaic an occasion? Can the event of Christ really be in such an everyday happening? Of all the ways in which a majestic God might disclose Himself, does this not seem the least promising? Can so much really hinge on so little?

No wonder preaching is called audacious! The miracle of all miracles is that despite these worldly, ordinary, earthbound circumstances God is pleased to speak through the ministry of his servant. What a tremendous thought! What a stupendous act! What a great calling, to be the instrument, the voice, the mouthpiece, where in such ordinary circumstances Almighty God, Creator of heaven and earth, is pleased to make himself known to his people in worship! This alone is enough to drive the preacher to his knees in gratitude and humility for the responsibility that is his by the grace of God.

Responsibility of the People

Of course, there is another aspect to the temerity of preaching corresponding to the unprecedented claims of the preacher. I refer obviously to the responsibility of the hearers, the people who sit in the pews. They play a vital role also in the dramatic event of preaching. Preaching or good teaching is basically a matter of *communication.* It is a two-way proposition, primarily a one-to-one relationship. There is no real teaching until the pupils have learned. Preaching as an act is incomplete until lives have been transformed, which transformation is precipitated by hearing, understanding, believing, and receiving the message from the man of God. No preacher has fully preached until someone has received the message from God and has experienced the worship experience.

At least the following several elements are included in the responsibility of the people who hear the preaching from the pulpit. First of all there must be *expectation.* The power of a great expectation cannot be overemphasized. The preacher's greatest error would be to underestimate the potentiality of the moment of preaching. If he does not expect God to speak through his Word, how in the world can the people maintain an atmosphere of such expectation? But the people must believe and expect God to speak, not only through the formal sermon but through the entire ministry of their pastor, the man of God, the minister of the gospel. The preacher here, as in so many instances, sets the pattern for the congregation in creating an atmosphere of expectancy. This is the key to the worship experience.

Secondly there must be the aspect of *recollection*, or remembering. One of the greatest aids to worship is the faculty of memory, the ability to recall our blessings as well as the central truths of our faith. The psalmist has well said, "Bless the Lord, O my soul, and forget not all his benefits." One reason for the emphasis in the Scripture on thanksgiving is demonstrated in the value received from recounting our blessings. If we count our blessings, naming them one by one, recalling the great events that God has done for us in Jesus Christ, we are well on the way to overcoming the secular barrier in the minister-people relationship.

Perhaps the gravest significance of the church ordinances, baptism and the Lord's Supper, is just at this point of remembering the central event of the Christian faith. It is no accident that the ordinances centered around the cross of Christ, which is the focal point in God's relationship to man. Christian worship will become vital and vibrant as we magnify the occasions through music, Scripture, sermon, invitation, offering, and all the rest to recollect, to remember the great events of redemption. When the prophets of the Old Testament desired to bring the nation of Israel back to God, they inevitably recounted God's mighty acts in history, especially as centering around the great redemptive event of the exodus.

Thirdly, there is the element of *exposure*. This is what Bartlett calls the "public privacy of the pew." Preaching is basically a one-to-one relationship (as stated above), although it is obviously one of the mass media of communication. Jesus taught us that the most effective preaching even when facing multitudes is to one person. More effective is the preaching when the preacher by the grace of God can obliterate himself so that the hearer feels a personal and exclusive confrontation between his own heart and the living God. Phillips Brooks' classic statement concerning preaching as divine truth through human personality is still quite apropos.

Of course the message delivered must be capable of personal application by the varied assortment of individuals in the congregation. However, it must not be so personal as to be revealing or to indicate betrayal of confidences shared in the minister's counseling sessions. Each member of the congregation should be able to see *himself* exposed in the message but not other people, at least as far as specific shortcomings or needs are concerned.

Fourthly, there is the circumstance of *loving*. If the atmosphere of *agape* (love) does not exist between the preacher and his people, the people will not only fail to receive the message of God, but the preacher will fail in his task of propagating the message. Jesus said in John 13:35: "By this shall all men know that ye are my disciples, if ye have love one to another." The one unmistakable evidence of our being genuine disciples of Jesus is that we demonstrate Godlike love for fellow Christians within the household of faith. It is an audacious, perhaps a presumptuous claim that the preacher and his people make, namely, that God can and does choose to speak in such humble circumstances with the result of transformation of human life. But mark it well. Unless there is the atmosphere of love, respect, and genuine fellowship or New Testament *koinonia* the message from God will not be communicated.

The Main Thing

Of course there is much more to the minister's life and ministry than just preaching, but this is *the main thing.* The preacher is a preacher first! If God has called us to preach, then despite all of our multitudinous responsibilities we cannot forego our commitment to this main task! This concept of the temerity of preaching convinces me that the time has come to reemphasize, reclaim, and magnify afresh the role of the modern minister as a preacher.

Perhaps it is the result of so much pressure to produce in so many other areas, but tragically the call to *preach* has somehow lost its priority within the ministry in this day and age. There is an overwhelming need for rediscovering the thrill, the power, the challenge of standing up in the public place to speak for God! In my opinion nothing in the minister's busy life and schedule of events should ever be allowed to take precedence over the responsibility of being a preacher of God's truth!

Of course it is imperative that in the act of preaching the minister must dare to be himself! He must avoid the molds of the times. A God-called preacher is always unique. There is none other just like him. He has a distinct style, definite mannerisms, and a specific type of delivery. Thank God he is second to none *unless he attempts to imitate one of his peers!* The preacher must accept the validity of his call to preach with such devotion and clarity that he will studiously avoid imitation of others, ministerial whining, a special tone of voice, timeworn cliches, and obvious phrases.

This is no time for preachers to imitate each other, for no one else can do as effectively as you what God has called only you to do.

Prophet or Pastor?

One of my seminary professors, Clyde T. Francisco, has consistently reminded young preachers of the strategic differences between the prophetic and pastoral roles of the minister. Some preachers apparently feel compelled to preach like Amos, except that they are never quite prepared for the kind of response which Amos received! It is true that the minister must speak the truth, but he must always *speak the truth in love.* The modern-day minister must be more than a prophet thundering out the truth regardless of the circumstances. He must also be the pastor, the shepherd, the loving counselor, the patient confessor.

There is indeed a great need for renewed prophetic preaching in view of modern situations. But there is also a tremendous need for *pastoral preaching and ministry* in this confused and bewildered age. What ever happened to the loving, compassionate, caring concern of the man of God *for his people,* despite who they are or what they have become? We need more Jeremiahs today who are unafraid to weep over the sins of the people and nation, rather than just Amoses to pronounce unequivocal judgment and doom.

It is my opinion that it takes far more bravery, courage, and patience for the modern-day pastor to stick with his people when they often reflect unchristian attitudes and deep-seated prejudices than it does to thunder forth with prophetic pronouncements from the pulpit which would precipitate an almost immediate departure. It often takes more patience and fortitude (I repeat) to remain in a given place of service and to prayerfully, lovingly teach, to hope, to wait, and pray rather than precipitate a crisis which will result in a resignation either voluntary or forced.

Of course it is possible for the pastor to so magnify the pastoral role that he loses sight of his prophetic responsibilities. It is not either-or, but both. The prophetic proclamation of an unpopular truth in the tradition of Amos, coupled with the loving, compassionate, pastoral concern of the tender shepherd, is essential in the modern ministry. The pastor who neglects either or both of these aspects of the ministry does so to his own detriment. The clearer the relationship between these two roles in his own heart and life the easier it will be for him to make decisions on what he feels he should speak out on and what issues he should attack more indirectly.

Yes, preaching is a presumptuous, perhaps foolish, certainly audacious and temerous responsibility. But this does not mean the preacher should act foolishly or irresponsibly. There is a great difference between the foolishness of the preaching and preaching foolishly! Of course, only the minister himself can finally decide what constitutes the difference as far as he personally is concerned. Perhaps diligent study habits and careful preparation will assist us in this all important matter.

V

Studying and Sermonizing

From the lofty claims of preaching as an act of God through human instrumentality to responsive people, we now come to the *practical* aspects of preaching. We now grapple with the problem of the minister's study habits, sermon preparation, and Bible study. These may appear mundane and unexciting, but their significance is paramount. No more fatal mistake could be made by the minister than to presume that since preaching involves an act of God, little or no human preparation is required. In fact the opposite is the case. Because God Almighty is involved in the preaching event it behooves us to give diligent attention to study and preparation for the high and holy hour.

Often I have been asked to explain how I prepare my sermons. No doubt every preacher has been asked this question many times. It is not easily answered, however, for no preacher prepares all sermons the same way. In fact most preachers will hesitate to publicly relate all the ways and means whereby sermon ideas, outlines, and messages come to him and are subsequently developed. Nevertheless there is value in reviewing basic patterns of sermon preparation.

Primarily I have always been an expository preacher. This does not mean that every sermon or even necessarily that most of my sermons follow the formal textbook definition of an expository sermon. But even the topical sermons often have units of Scripture exposition contained within them. The points in my messages are quite frequently substantiated by various Scripture references. This has always been my pattern, no doubt springing from early childhood and that innermost, eager desire to know and make known the Bible and its message. This means that automatically the primary source for my sermon preparation is systematic Bible study. This is not the kind of Bible study that is done in preparation for a specific message, but preferably a systematic verse by verse study in depth of some book in the Bible. This is unquestionably the best background for regular expository preaching.

Since the early days of the first pastorate I have frequently conducted Bible conferences in all my pastorates. I still remember the quite remarkable first Bible conference conducted in the first pastorate. It was quite an ambitious undertaking to say the least. Two hours of exposition in the mornings and two hours in the evenings were designated for the study of the epistle to the Hebrews and the epistle to the Romans respectively. I had only a couple of commentaries plus my Bible. But for weeks I studied and then taught for four hours a day for five consecutive days. Physical exhaustion so overwhelmed me that it was necessary to teach the last session while sitting in a chair! But out of that verse-by-verse exposition in Hebrews and Romans came literally hundreds of outlines, texts, sermon ideas, possible subjects and/or topics. After more than twenty-three years of preaching I have found this still to be the best single source for sermon ideas and suggestions.

How Prepare Sermons?

Since most of my preaching is expository, usually the first thing in the preparation of a sermon is selecting the Scripture passage. This comes either because of a specific passage which lends itself to sermonizing and exposition, or because a particular passage fits a general subject or material on which I plan to speak. So the process might be outlined as follows:

(1) Determining the *passage* and/or *subject*. A notebook or file folder for loose sheets serves admirably as a storehouse for sermon ideas. These are readily available when needed most and can serve as a catalytic agent when thoughts and ideas are slow in coming.

(2) *Studying* the passage again *in depth* through all available commentaries and books in my library. I have been able through the years to acquire a considerable library of good expositions of Scripture. I prefer single commentaries on specific books of the Bible rather than sets of commentaries or books of sermons. My library has only a few volumes of printed sermons.

(3) The *outline* normally is developed during the course of the studies in the commentaries and the Scripture passage itself. Seldom have I ever studied through all the commentaries and books in my library on a particular passage of Scripture without having an outline literally jump out at me. Usually two or three alternatives present themselves also. Thus by the time the intensive study is completed for the particular passage I have written down several outlines and ideas.

(4) If many volumes are being used the next step involved is making *notations* on the temporary outline. These notations might include outline subpoints, developmental ideas, possible illustrative material, and so forth. This scrap paper eventually will be thrown away.

(5) *Illustrations* are next. If they are not readily available or have not come to mind from experiences of the past in the course of the Bible study, I search. Books of illustrations have limited value, but occasionally may provide just the right experience. Some books of sermons are valuable only because of the illustrative material they contain.

It is my habit *never to tell a story unless the story really illustrates* the point. For that reason I am not known as a storyteller preacher. This is not to deprecate those who obviously have gifts in this area. My forte unquestionably is Scripture exposition, although many great preachers of today are master storytellers as well as masterful preachers. Of course there are many ways to illustrate other than telling a story. Word pictures, figures of speech, terse reminders of coming events all serve to illustrate biblical truth but without the severe penalty of occupying too much time. In my opinion if the story is remembered but the truth is forgotten, the illustration would have been better left out.

(6) Then comes the *introduction* and *conclusion*. These two are the most important parts of the sermon. They need far more careful attention and preparation than is usually realized. For me, they are almost always carefully memorized. The opening statement and the conclusion will probably be longer remembered by the people who hear the sermon than the intriguing outline, catchy phrases, or unusual illustrations. What the preacher says in the beginning will determine whether or not some people will listen further,

and what he says in conclusion (especially the *way* the sermon is concluded) will determine whether or not it was worth listening to!

(7) Next comes the actual *writing* down of *portions* of the message including the introduction and conclusion, the basic outline, and several pivotal points. It is not my habit to write out messages in full. In fact when I do write out the message in full it is usually done after the sermon has been delivered. I do make copious notes which are carefully filed and can be found either through the topic, Scripture text, or the subject matter in my index file. It is a ridiculous waste of time and energy to fail to appropriately file sermonic material for future use. No matter how sparse the outline or written material and notes, whatever has been written down should be readily available whenever the same subject or text is to be utilized again.

Preaching Without Notes

After this particular procedure has been followed, however, the sermon is not nearly ready to preach. For many years I have refused to take a written outline into the pulpit with me at the time of the sermon. In the early years of my ministry notes were always present in the pulpit but were seldom referred to. Already, I had worked to master the material and was quite familiar with everything there. I became convinced, during seminary days, of the necessity for taking another hour or two of sermon preparation in order to master the outline and the brief notes. Constant eye-to-eye contact could then be maintained while standing in the pulpit. The thing that convicted me was that I would spend endless hours memorizing reams of material, textbooks, notebooks, dates, historical events, simply to make an A in a given course. Why should I not be willing to spend a little extra time to master a few pages of written material in order to be completely free and at my best in the pulpit?

Of course I am not suggesting that this would be the best method for everyone. There are some men who relate that they would simply panic if they did not have a hidden crutch to lean upon in an emergency. I would not be critical of these. Many of them are much better preachers than I. I am simply saying that for me it is much better to master the material, memorize the outline, and perhaps mark a few passages in the Bible using tabs or gem clips. After carefully reviewing the message in my own mind in a prayerful attitude, I can stand before the people in the pulpit and preach extemporaneously what I can remember.

Often I am asked if I do not forget something. Of course the answer must be in the affirmative. Some things are left out, some things that I thought were very important! Sometimes I am chagrined to check my notes after preaching to see that I omitted a certain passage or idea, but my rationale is that if it did not make enough impression on me to remember it, then perhaps it was best left out of the sermon at the time! I have long since become convinced that the Lord is not nearly as interested as we seem to be in our people hearing all the things we think that are important. This kind of creative extemporaneity has provided me a vital element of freedom in the pulpit that has contributed immeasurably to my continued enchantment with the unique event of preaching.

The All-Important Idea

Of course there are many other ways to begin a sermon. In recent years for instance, current issues of the day have played a prominent part in my preaching messages. For instance, I recently preached a sermon entitled "New Hearts and Heart Transplants" giving what I believe to be a Christian approach toward the problems of transplantations of physical organs of the human body. There has recently been a message on space exploration with particular reference to the epistles to the Colossians and Hebrews. These epistles actually have quite a bit to say about Christ and space.

Also, I am quite fond of delivering *series of sermons.* From others I have received the idea of sermon series on great nights of the Bible, great doctrines of the faith, people who met Jesus in a personal encounter, a series on Communism, on Christology, revival sermons, and of course sermons for special days. Fourth of July and Labor Day have been the occasion for messages on church and state, the Christian in politics, the dignity of labor, and so forth. These are issues and events people are thinking about naturally because of the season or holiday. Why should not the preacher magnify and capitalize on the existing interests of Christmas time, for instance, by preaching on the Incarnation of Christ or the meaning of the virgin birth, instead of deploring the commercialization of these holidays? Why should we not magnify the biblical truths and Christian revelation which are identified with these particular days?

Of course I am greatly indebted to other preachers and speakers for many sermon ideas. Many times while listening to a sermon or lecture I have received an idea for a sermon completely extraneous to the context of what the speaker was saying. A new insight came almost by accident. Yet I believe this to be by providence. Cultivating the attitude and habit of being a good listener is apparently not only a virtue but has the practical value of assisting the busy minister in acquiring and even developing sermon ideas.

Sometimes these ideas come in the middle of the night. Insomnia has produced some of the most creative thoughts in the entire lives of us preachers! The important thing to remember here is that whether it is in the middle of the night or listening to a formal sermon or lesson, when the idea comes, *jot it down.* Write down enough so that you will remember what it is. A word or phrase or two may not be sufficient weeks later. Most of us have wasted our best thoughts by failing to record them and being unable to recall them later. There is no substitute for taking full advantage of those rare moments of inspiration in the realm of sermonic ideas. Remember, write it down or most probably you will not remember it!

The Preacher at His Best

There is no greater thrill to the preacher than preaching. And yet the thrill of preaching is what makes the preparation so exciting. I can study diligently and for long hours, realizing that the reward comes primarily in the activity of proclaiming the message in the power of the Spirit. To remember an exciting moment in preaching can inspire the thoughtful preacher to many hours of biblical and sermonic research in anticipation of the next crowning event!

When Sunday night comes around and the last sermon for the day has been delivered, I am often anxiously awaiting next Sunday's opportunities. It is a thrill to have preached victoriously and then to look forward eagerly to next Sunday's sermons. Sunday night in our services the next Sunday's sermon topics are often publicly announced. The Scripture text is given, the topic announced, and the appetites of the people whetted. If the minister is excited about his preaching responsibilities, the people will be also!

My sermon topics are listed from three to six months in advance and made available to the minister of music and the minister of education. These are always subject to last minute alterations or substitutions, but I have long found it quite helpful to prepare the preaching schedule several months, even a year, in advance. Of course (as previously indicated) every preacher needs a creative file where ideas, helps, illustrations, outlines, and other tidbits can be collected. Periodically going through this particular file can add immeasurably to the anticipated sermon topics for the future.

Preaching from the Overflow

Years ago I heard a talk about an old preacher's concept of preaching from the overflow. He described it as an artesian well or flowing well where the water flows steadily but the great reservoir of water underneath the earth resting in a basin of nonporous rock was unseen. If the well flows year in and year out in a small stream one can rest assured that there are many hundreds of thousands of gallons of water underneath the earth that are never seen. The old preacher compared this well with the responsibilities of studying and preaching.

The preacher like the poet must literally be a part of all that he has met. This includes everything that he sees and reads, the local daily newspaper, periodicals and magazines, popular novels, business reports, as well as denominational literature, Bible commentaries, and theological treatises. I shall never forget the advice that an interim pastor in my church gave me as a teen-age boy when I asked him to recommend some books to read. His suggestion was, "Read everything you can get your hands on!" I did not understand that as much then as I think I do now. I believe I can honestly say that I have not read anything that has not been of some benefit in some way, either negatively or positively, in sermon preparation. In general reading, sermons often pop out, ideas come, even outlines are suggested. Again they must be jotted down so they will be useful in the future. Reading is one of my hobbies and although the limitations of time greatly curtail my normal inclinations it seems that I can always make time for some reading, because this is the real storehouse of information and knowledge.

If the seminary student during the days of his educational pursuits does not cultivate the habit of extensive reading over and above and beyond the bare requirements of the courses, it will be most difficult if not impossible to develop such habits after seminary days amidst pressing demands of the pastorate. The point is you cannot wait *until there is plenty of time to learn to study.* Reading and studying must be a part of the minister's life from the very beginning. Just as he cannot afford to wait until after seminary days to learn to preach, so the young preacher and the college or seminary student cannot wait until after graduation to learn to read and become adept at filling his mind and heart and soul with things out of which he can build sermons.

Preaching is literally from the overflow. If we do not keep filling our minds and hearts with information, knowledge, inspiration, and so forth, then the well will eventually run dry. There is nothing any drier than a dry sermon drawn from a dry well because there are no hidden reservoirs or streams of living water flowing within!

Sermonic Ethics

In preparing to preach the minister must keep several basic presuppositions in mind. These are points to remember, principles to revolve or rotate around, polarizations if you please of sermonic ethics. They are the results of my own observations, and they are certainly subject to revision. Of course the words are arbitrarily chosen, but I believe I can explain what is meant by each one.

First of all the preacher's sermon should be *nonindividualistic but personal.* There can be no betrayal of confidences from the pulpit. The preacher must carefully avoid singling out an individual in the congregation so that he is identified by the other members of the congregation or by himself. I am reminded of the young couple that came to my study for personal counseling in regard to their marriage. They began by requesting and receiving a solemn commitment from me that their particular case would never be used in a sermon illustration either here or elsewhere. This made me wonder how many people during the course of the telling of an illustration have vowed privately never to call on that minister for advice and counsel about personal matters!

Yet the sermons must be personal to the point that each one who listens can feel that God is speaking to him in a particular way. There is a difference, however, in isolating an individual case or betraying a confidence and in preaching in such a way that the people can feel that the minister is divinely guided in the preparation of his message. The choice of words may be arbitrary but the idea seems best expressed in the terms, nonindividualistic but personal.

Secondly, the sermon must be *nonacademic but studious.* By this is meant that the sermon should reflect diligent study and preparation, but not be overly erudite. How easy it is for a well trained, theologically oriented minister in his field to use unfamiliar terminology in the name of scholarship, but to the deletion of communication! Let us remember that we are not speaking to seminary classrooms, but that we are speaking to the congregation that represents a cross section of the community. All ages, varying educational backgrounds, and different emotional and spiritual levels of growth and development are represented. Our sermons must not sound like academic discussions but should definitely reflect the long hours of tedious preparation, diligent study, and earnest prayer that precedes each delivery. If the songs from the choir are in Latin and the preacher in the pulpit speaks Greek, no wonder our people are turning to speaking in tongues!

Thirdly, the sermon must be *nonpolitical but relevant.* Of course the Christian should be interested in and involved in politics. Yet the minister must be reminded that he is to speak out on the moral issues, not the political factions of his day. To take a stand on a moral issue in the community inevitably involves one in civic controversy and political accusations. The minister must rise above and keep himself above the low level of personal retaliation. He must speak to the issues of the day where there is an issue and where moral and spiritual principles are involved.

Unfortunately we seemingly have a gift of speaking out on the irrelevant and the non-crucial. Seventy-five years ago there was a heated debate between two Baptist pastors in Atlanta, Georgia, on the morality of females riding bicycles in public. We seem to still have this marvelous ability to magnify the really vital matters!

Of course there comes a time when a minister must take a

stand regardless of the consequences. Just be sure when we take this stand that it is a stand worth taking, and above all that it is a stand on an issue that is important enough to take such a stand on!

Preaching ought to be the preacher's finest hour regardless of his personality, his adeptness in the sickroom, his comforting ministry in time of bereavement and sorrow, his counseling to the troubled and the disturbed, his ability to promote, to organize, to minister. He ought to be at his very best when he stands behind the sacred desk to break the bread of life. He is first and foremost a preacher, but preachers are not born, they are made. The preacher with the help, strength, and grace of God can in a sense *make himself* by serious study of the Scriptures, earnest prayer, continuous searching for the Spirit-filled life, and determination to do his very best under God. These are strategic tasks and not easily attainable goals, but the trumpets in the morning are calling to the ministers of our day to come to the pulpits of our churches and give us a word from God!

VI

The Strategic Role of the Layman

Thank God for the laymen in the four churches I have served as pastor! In more than twenty-three years of preaching and having served in four different pastorates, I have only the most pleasant of memories as far as pastor-laymen relationships are concerned.

These men have been the most dedicated men I have ever known, by and large. My attitude is that of the apostle Paul toward the Philippians, "For I thank my God upon every remembrance of you." My ministry has been enhanced and my life and friendships enriched as a result of the spiritual influence and leadership of these humble servants of the church and of the Lord. A salute to the laymen is definitely in order!

Of course other ministers have reported adverse circumstances and bitter experiences with deacons and laymen in various churches in the past and in the present. One need not search long or far for ready examples of strained deacon-pastor relationships or even instances of major blowups. I am not questioning the validity of these reports nor suggesting any percentages in regard to how many churches have deacon-pastor relationship problems. It is simply my wish to record my own pleasant and desirable-to-recollect experiences with the laymen in the churches I have served. I can honestly say that the relationships between pastor and deacons and/or laymen of my four pastorates have been delightful, spiritual, and I believe mutually profitable, relationships.

It would be well-nigh impossible to give credit where all of it is due for the indelible impressions for good and for God made upon my life by godly men of the churches that I have served. They have given me inspiration when I was discouraged. They have followed my leadership when I have challenged them. I have leaned heavily upon them for counsel, advice, suggestions, and by and large they have never failed. Of one thing I am assuredly confident. My ministry would not be what it is today without these Christian laymen, and whatever degree of success I might have attained is directly related to the spirituality, leadership, and personal support of these men.

For instance, I can recall being deeply indebted to a dedicated Christian layman who literally taught me how to visit during my first pastorate. He spent endless hours of his time going with me from house to house. He introduced me to people, as well as to methods of church work and organization. He never complained or suggested we slack off on the extended schedule of persistent visitation. Many times during personal prayer, I have included a special prayer of thanksgiving for this man who gave so freely of his time to this young preacher. Who would have taught me with such patience and thoroughness had not this layman been a pliable and expendable instrument in the Master's hands?

In one of my pastorates I was not the moderator of the church, although I had been raised in an environment where the pastor was always the moderator of the church. The godly deacon who had been elected moderator of his congregation was the epitomy of patience, poise, and perseverance. I learned far more from him because he was the moderator than I would have felt the need to learn if I had been the moderator. His contributions to my life and ministry are unquestionable, and I shall be eternally grateful.

In my last two pastorates it has been my privilege to lead the deacons and laymen of the churches to participate in a churchwide visitation ministry whereby on several occasions during one Sunday afternoon the entire membership of the particular church was visited in the interest of the individual church program. Of course I have also served in evangelism with an evangelistic team for approximately two years. Part of my responsibility was to lead deacons and laymen in such visitation programs of the entire church membership in the interest of the forthcoming revival.

The logistics of such a one-day visitation of the entire church membership are simple and not particularly time consuming. The church membership must be divided into family units and divided thusly into equal in number groups for assignment and visitation purposes. If a church has three hundred resident family units, then thirty laymen would be needed to contact ten homes or families each on a given Sunday afternoon. If such a church had only ten deacons then each one would need to enlist two additional laymen in advance of the scheduled time of visitation. If it would be desirable to visit in teams of two, then either sixty men would need to be enlisted or each team would be responsible for contacting twenty families.

The greatest single truth that I have learned from these

visitation programs is that the work of the church of today as in New Testament days cannot be carried on without involving laymen. These men are the key to any pastor's program and they must be given opportunity for leadership. They give most of the money. They provide the primary leadership. They have most of the creative ideas. They are the ones who will be upset if the pastor makes mistakes. They are the ones who will be quickest to praise if the program and work are going well. Why not challenge them with meaningful avenues of fruitful activity? Men will respond to a real challenge.

No doubt many problems between pastors and deacons and/or laymen are brought about by the attitude of stubbornness so frequently observable on the part of the pastor. It may stem from a deep sense of inadequacy on the pastor's part. The minister must studiously guard himself against being obsequious for he will never be able to challenge any layman worth his salt to positive Christian leadership and service by trying in effect to bribe to obtain the desired results. Laymen quickly see through pretension and ulterior motives on the part of the pastor. Nothing short of absolute sincerity and genuineness will suffice to enlist laymen in the responsible tasks of the church's life.

Admits He Is Wrong

Now my basic philosophy as a minister of the gospel in regard to pastor-layman relationships is this: It should not be too difficult for the minister of all people *to admit on occasion that he is wrong!* It is true that our churches by and large put the minister on a pedestal. It is often hard to consciously bring oneself down from this elevated position, but there is nothing that will lift the minister higher in the esteem and respect of the congregation than for him to reveal the fact that he is *human,* he is flesh and blood, that he makes mistakes just like others do, and that he is not too proud to apologize, to confess, and ask forgiveness. I can remember an experience when because of the pressures of time and other circumstances I plunged headlong into what became an exceedingly involved emotional and controversial issue. It was too late to back out when the emotional reaction was discovered but I shall never forget the experience of publicly apologizing to the deacons. Their response to the project was more enthusiastic and exciting than any I had ever dreamed possible even from the beginning! Laymen will not reject the pastor who admits he was wrong and apologizes. Just the opposite is true. They will love and respect him even more for his integrity and manliness.

My mind was made up a long time ago that I would never do anything through my church "around" the deacons. I would either lead them or drop the program. Many times I have told these godly men, "I am a deacon-dependent type pastor. You may get along without *me,* but I cannot get along without *you.*" And this is reflective of my sincerest beliefs. If as pastor I cannot lead, inspire, and command the respect of the deacons, then to at least some degree I have forfeited my leadership over the congregation as a whole. After all, the deacons are a *part of the congregation,* and a substantial part at that.

My father is a deacon and my brother is a deacon. Both of these men have served as chairmen of pulpit committees in their respective churches. I remember some delightful and humorous incidents related by my father as a lad at home upon his return from pulpit committee journeys. (Someday

I would like to write a book about pulpit committees!) I think the Lord has used this to give me insights, not only into pastor-pulpit committee relationships but pastor-deacon-layman relationships as well. Deacons and other laymen are human; they have problems, heartaches, frustrations, and failures just as preachers do. Preachers need to understand this just like they expect laymen to understand it about preachers.

Mr. Chairman

In the course of my present pastorate I have had the privilege of serving with eight different men as chairman of deacons. It has been my practice never to interfere or to become involved whatsoever by suggestion or overt act or word to effect or deny the election of any man to the office of the chairman of deacons. In my opinion this is the highest office that a layman can fill in my church. But I believe sincerely that I can cooperate with and work with any man who is elected chairman by the forty-five active deacons in our congregation. If I as pastor cannot cooperate with and work effectively with the man whom forty-four other deacons have elected as chairman then the inescapable conclusion must be that the fault lies within the pastor rather than the deacons! Surely we can trust the Spirit of God to give direction in the election of deacon officers as well as in the election and ordination of men to the deaconship by the congregation.

Immediately after the election of the deacon officers for the new church year it has been my practice to meet with the newly elected chairman and to explain to him my complete and utter confidence in his advice, suggestions, criticisms, leadership, and counsel. It would sometimes prove fatal to wait until a moment of crisis appears to attempt to establish rapport with the deacon chairman. He is my right arm as far as church administration goes, and I will not lose the first opportunity to assure him of my cooperation as well as interdependence, thus cementing significant and enduring relationships.

During a recent evangelistic crusade, the evangelistic team originally scheduled could not come, and the pastor and the minister of music were invited to conduct the service. The chairman of our deacons presided in every service. He made the announcements, led in prayer, received the offering, did everything except sing and preach. His was a strategic role of dynamic leadership. It not only served to provide him an opportunity in significant service, but enhanced the unique and permanent role of the pastor in the eyes of the people as well.

Opportunities for Service

The laymen in my church have a serious responsibility because they have frequent opportunity to give dynamic spiritual leadership to the pastor and staff as well as to the entire church family. The Deacon-led Spiritual Growth Program has provided continuing opportunities for the development of lay leadership. Regular, rotational deacon-led invocations in every Sunday morning worship service and brief preservice prayer meetings involving all ordained men serve a multiplicity of useful ends. If the best in service and dedication is to be produced in our deacons then more must be required of them than serving the Lord's Supper and conducting the canvassing program to culminate the stewardship drive.

Let me repeat again that it is imperative for the pastor in the church of today to be man enough to admit that he can make mistakes, and to apologize when he has obviously been in the wrong. The laymen will love such a pastor even more, not less. God give us the grace to be man enough to admit what we all know already in advance! Frequently deacons and laymen mention the fact that preachers are almost always complaining. We complain about overwork, too many other responsibilities, so many demands, not enough time, how many calls that have to be made in the middle of the night, how many sermons have to be preached and other duties performed.

After careful reflection I am convinced that the average preacher who speaks so frequently about his many responsibilities within the limitations of time is not doing so primarily to complain about what he is doing. Most preachers love their work and would not trade places with anybody in the world. They are simply attempting to share with somebody (and in this case the laymen) the knowledge of how diverse and multitudinous the activities and responsibilities of a minister really are.

There is a basic need inherent in every minister to share with someone else something of the wide range of activities involved in the ministry. It is a desire for humility on his part that keeps him from boasting about these things. So the next best thing is simply to report them negatively *as if* they were burdens and *as if* the activities were too burdensome and pressing. It is simply a mechanism or device for telling someone about the varied and abundant activities in the daily life of a minister.

No preacher would be as easily discouraged or defeated if he could feel that others knew and appreciated what he was doing. There is a basic need for every minister to understand that somebody knows and cares. Perhaps some layman who reads this can realize the strategic role he could occupy in growing a bigger and better minister by simply asking him (the minister) what he has been doing. It must be done, however, in a way not to imply that he (the layman) thinks the minister has been lazy or inactive, but as an expression of genuine interest and godly concern.

Prayer Retreat

Recently the deacons, who number almost a hundred at the First Baptist Church in Dothan, participated in a prayer retreat. At the conclusion of this two-day retreat, as pastor I was invited to deliver the closing message on what it means to be a deacon in First Baptist Church in a day like today. I began by saying it obviously is a time for changing our traditional and outdated concepts of the deaconship. The New Testament principles of deaconship and the qualifications for deaconship are spelled out quite clearly, but beyond this there are few guidelines except our own experience and the leadership of the Holy Spirit as to what it means to be a deacon in our church today. The time has come for a new exploration of the role and ministry of a deacon in a twentieth century church.

My first suggestion (along the line of the changing role of the deacon) was that the deacon today can *no longer merely mechanically attend the monthly meetings* and perform a few other perfunctory duties such as receiving the offering, serving the Lord's Supper, and so forth as he has done perhaps in the past. The deacon today must be a *minister* and a *servant* in the truest New Testament sense. Our Junior age daughter recently engaged in a heated conversation in a Training Union group over whether or not the pastor was a servant. She vociferously maintained that her daddy was not anybody's servant! Of course she misunderstood the New Testament concept of service. The pastor *is* a servant, but the deacon is also a servant. The word for deacon means service and ministry, and fortunately the concept of the modern deacon involves his sharing in the pastor's ministry.

Second, the deacon of today can *no longer simply endorse automatically the pastor's program.* The deacon must launch out creatively and carry through on his own ideas. He may approve the pastor's suggestions and follow his leadership, but the deacon can no longer afford the luxury of relegating the initiation of all church programs to the pastor and staff alone. A classic example of this was our deacons' prayer retreat itself. This idea was conceived and implemented by the chairman of deacons, his officers, and a few committee chairmen whom he appointed, by and large without the involvement of the pastor until the actual time of the retreat. It is not enough simply to follow the pastor's leadership. The deacons and laymen have a responsibility as leaders themselves!

Third, more than ever, in the midst of a perverse world, the deacon must *shine as a moral light amidst the darkness.* It must not be spoken among you, I suggested to our deacons, that there is immorality, dishonesty, unethical business practices, and so forth. The church is still standing upon a steeple as it were in the community, and a critical and impatient world is consistently searching for inconsistency and hypocrisy within the church. It may be true that the church has been brought into disrepute because of the moral laxity and unethical conduct of some of her ministers. But it is equally important for laymen to hold high the standards of Jesus Christ and manifest daily to the world a life of soberness, godliness, and Christian charity.

Fourth, the deacon of today must *maintain a deep spiritual and devotional life.* It is not enough for a man to be a good businessman, with financial resources, good contacts, and all the rest, if he is not a man of the Spirit, a man of the Book, and a man of prayer. A deacon above all must be a spiritual man, not just a financial one.

In short the deaconship can mean to a man just what he wants it to mean. He can make his pastor a better man, make his church a better church, or he can contribute to dissension, division, and the pastor's personal frustration. I am happy to testify that the deacons and laymen that I have known and with whom I have served have done the positive and the big thing, and have made my ministry what it is today.

VII

Calling Out the Called

This is *the day of youth* in America and in the world. Of this there can be no question. More than half the population in the United States is now under twenty-five years of age. An increasing birth rate and an increasing life-span both contribute to the ever increasing percentage of our total population that would be classified as *young people.* Youth are on the increase both in numbers and in influence as well, in our nation and in the entire world.

We are seeing the result of this youth oriented population explosion on every hand. College and university campus riots and hippy-happenings dramatically illustrate the crisis of our day. Increasing demands are being made on adult society, traditional mores, and the establishment. The threat of the downfall of our political and economic system is now quite real. "Don't trust anyone over thirty" is not nearly as amusing now as when I first heard it!

More youth means more challenge to the status quo, more rejection of tradition, authority, and previous sacred cows. The new generation is not content to hear the pat answers to the pressing problems which we have inherited from the generations of the past. There must be a more intelligent grasping of the issues of the day, a clearer identification of what the issues really are, and a reasonable attempt to hear youth speak to the issues and suggest their own possible solutions. One of the reasons the modern youth rebellion has taken so violent a turn is no doubt due to the fact that this is apparently the only way many youth can get the ear of the nation!

Of course this increasing youthful population is of vital concern to the church. We can overlook this element only to our own doom. It may already be too late. Of course the thesis of this book suggests optimism and you have perhaps already guessed that I believe that the energy of today's youth *can* be harnassed for Christ and through the church in an unprecedented way. I do not acquiesce to the charge that old-fashioned, biblically-authoritative, Christ-centered Christianity is outmoded and irrelevant to the needs and demands of today's youth. To the contrary that is exactly what American youth and the youth of the world need today more than ever before!

Do Something for Youth

Have you ever heard someone say, "Why doesn't this church do something for the young people?" Well of course the young people are a part of the church. They *are* the church, at least those who have been saved and have been baptized into our fellowship. They have a responsibility to work and serve in the church and in the community just as the adults do. And yet we must give the youth *opportunities* for service, for they have long felt dominated and overshadowed by the adults. Why, for instance, should not responsible young people in our churches today serve on the finance committee, the church council, the music committee, all the regular standing committees of the church as well as the special Youth Week programs, Youth Retreats, and Student Nights? If we expect young people to serve then we must constantly take steps to insure that they are being provided with occasion for real, responsible service.

The truth is that many of these young people are eager to respond to demonstrate their maturity. They just need a chance! Many are eagerly awaiting the call to specific duty. One reason the youth on the outside are not any more responsive to our attempts to bring them inside is that they do not want to be like the young people they have already seen on the inside, that is, blind sheep moving in whatever direction they are driven by the adult shepherds! It may be that one of our most effective evangelistic ministries could be the more adequate utilization of our church youth in areas of responsibility and significance.

Of course, one of the most critical aspects in regard to young people-pastor relationships is in the area of church-related vocational service. As I have indicated previously there is no more challenging service in the world today than that of the gospel ministry. What greater possible service to our youth could be rendered in this day of uncertainty and turmoil than to lead them to completely dedicate their lives to the cause of Jesus Christ? And yet statistics alarmingly indicate a decrease in the numbers of young people in all denominations committing their lives to this type of ministry and service. It seems to me that the pastor occupies a strategic role in leading his church to call out the called.

Definition of Terms

Perhaps we need to begin with a definition of terms in the phrase "calling out the called." I believe this adequately expresses our concept and understanding of the divine call into church-related vocational service. We cannot call young people into God's service. God must call them. We believe in a God-called ministry. So the proper term is "*calling out* the called." We do not call them; God calls them, but it is the responsibility of the pastor and the church to *create the spiritual atmosphere* in which those who are being called by God can respond to that call, can hear it and accept it, and respond to it.

If God calls people into special church-related vocational service (as we believe that he does), and if there is a need for more workers today (and there is a shortage of such workers), then we can conclude, *not that God is failing to call* more and more of our young people into special service, but that *some are not hearing the call,* and *others,* hearing the call, *are not responding* to it. God is still calling enough to meet the need. But the need perhaps indicates that we have failed to create the spiritual atmosphere in our churches conducive to young people hearing the call, and hearing the call, responding to it with faith and commitment of their lives.

Somehow we have failed to call out the called and somehow we have been on the decline so far as the number of young people answering God's call for special church-related vocational service is concerned. There is a sparcity of detailed information and written specific helps for the minister, for the church, and for the young person who is earnestly striving to ascertain what the will of God is for his heart and life. Let me suggest three or four things that we can do as ministers and lead our churches to do as the people of God to help call out the called, or help create the atmosphere in which our young people will hear and respond in obedience to the divine call of God.

What We Can Do

First of all, *we need to preach on how to know the will of God, and explain what we mean by a divine call.* Perhaps one of the reasons why some of our youth are not responding positively to God's call is they do not understand what we mean by God's call. They have a complete misunderstanding sometimes of what it is or what it should be, and they are awaiting a lightning bolt, cataclysmic experience that they have heard someone else talk about, which may or may not be God's method for calling them into special church-related vocational services.

Now, I mentioned that there is a sparcity of helpful material, but a great light in the midst of this darkness is a scintillating little book by T. B. Maston entitled, *God's Will and Your Life,* which should be in every church library. This book deals for the most part with the totality of finding God's will in one's life, but a small portion of it deals with God's call for special church-related vocational service. Ministers need to suggest to the young people, as Dr. Maston does, that there are several tests that they can apply to themselves in helping them to understand, to ascertain, and to know the will of God for their lives.

How to Know the Will of God

Maston mentions among other things the test of *common sense,* which is a test, strangely enough, we often do not apply to the Lord's call. We apply it to everything else, but this is a test that we can apply also to an understanding of God's will for our lives vocationally. In addition to the test of common sense, there is the test of *conscience,* that is, how does one feel about it in the innermost heart and mind. Also there is the test of *counsel,* or advice and leadership, the shared experiences of others in conversations, counseling situations, and on the printed page. But most important of all is the test of the *will of Christ* sought through the Bible and prayer. What Jesus would have me to do is the acid test for ascertaining the will of God.

In addition there is the test of the *consent, or willingness of the individual.* I am reminded of what Jesus said in John 7:17, "If any man will do his will, he shall know of the doctrine, whether it be of God, or whether I speak of myself." A key to understanding God's will in your life is a *willingness to do that will whatever it is.* We must be willing not only to do what we think God may be leading us to do, but be willing to do anything else if God is calling us to do something else.

I have found it wise as a pastor in counseling young men who feel they may be called to the gospel ministry to ask them the question, "Are you willing to do *something else* if God is calling you to do something else? Are you just as willing to be a Christian businessman or a Christian doctor or a Christian schoolteacher, a layman in the church with Christ first in your life? Are you willing to do this if God is calling you to do this, as well as to preach?" A lot of times the assurance of the call to preach comes after a person says, "Lord, I am willing to preach, or I am willing to do anything else you might be calling me to do." But the will, the consent of the individual is important.

There is another test. It is the test of the *continuing nature* of the experience. I have talked to many who were called to preach and the majority of the men whom I know in the ministry relate that their call was not primarily a single cataclysmic, lightning bolt experience from the blue (which many of our young people seem to be expecting), but rather it was a growing, continuous, burning inner conviction that this is the will of God for me and for my life. This fact has revolutionized some people's understanding of the call of God for special service. *Most preachers relate that this sense of call was a quiet, growing realization within their heart and mind that God wanted them to do this particular thing!*

Now if this is our call to the ministry, why do we not explain this to our young people so they will know what to look for, and maybe we can avoid some of the confusion when one says, "I am willing to do the will of God, I just do not know what God wants me to do. God has not spoken to me clearly in the night as he did to Samuel, or in the light from heaven as he did to Saul on the road to Damascus." Perhaps if we would share more frequently our experience of the call to the ministry, and what we mean by a divine call, and how we came to understand that call in our lives, our young people would be far better prepared to hear and respond when God speaks to them.

Relating Conversion Experience

Then we should not only share with our young people our sense of divine call, but give our people, even those who have not been called to special church-related vocational service, an opportunity just to tell about their conversion to Christ. It is amazing, but most people cannot have a clear conception of a divine call for special service unless they have a clear conception of their conversion experience to begin with.

We have a practice in our church that you may find

helpful as far as the deacons are concerned. We have an examining council comparable to that of the examination council for a minister who is about to be ordained, for our deacons, even after they have been elected by the church. Before they are ordained, we call these newly elected deacons together with the other ordained deacons and give each one of them an opportunity to tell about their conversion experience, to tell about when they were saved, and about their initial profession of faith, and when they became a Baptist. It is amazing how this helps to solidify the consciousness of the call of God in one's life when you tell it yourself and when you hear others tell it.

Dedicated Christian Living

Secondly, if we are to create the atmosphere in which God can call out and the called can respond, *we must precede and lead our young people into the most dedicated Christian life possible.* Now think about it for a moment. When was the last time you witnessed a young person coming to commit his life to special service?

Every time a young person does that, just stop and think, what kind of young person is it? In my experience those who are answering God's call in my church are those who are among the most dedicated Christian young people in the church. Now, there may be exceptions to this, but most of the time those who are answering God's call are already among the most dedicated Christian young people I know. Is it not logical, therefore, if we are to help call out the called that we ought to first of all begin by trying to lead our young people into the most dedicated Christian life possible? And that means we ought to teach them the real meaning of discipleship.

A disciple is a disciplined, trained follower of Jesus Christ. The word "disciple" is related etymologically to the word "discipline." Most of the teachings of Jesus about discipleship in the New Testament do not refer to the *way* to become a disciple, but to the *strenuous requirements and discipline necessary for true discipleship!* Jesus warns us to count the cost before entering into such a spiritual endeavor.

Sometimes we are afraid we will drive our young people away by presenting the full and complete claims of Christ to their lives. But my experience has been the contrary; *young people are challenged by something that means something,* and I believe we will bring more of them closer to Christ by presenting the full claims of Christ to their lives, and the full meaning of being trained, disciplined followers of Jesus than we will ever drive away.

Then I believe we ought to be honest and frank with our young people. They can see through us. We can deceive everybody else in the church before the young people. Hypocrisy is abhorred by modern youth, and the problem is we are often building our straw men and creating problems in answering questions that none of our youth are even asking anymore! We are living in a bygone age. We are talking about things that were problems for our grandparents when today's youth are faced with the problems of the new morality, the playboy philosophy, the beat generation, the hippies, drug experimentation, and the popular temptations of a modern day. We had best understand their problems and speak their language or we shall lose this generation for Jesus Christ.

I believe we ought to speak frankly to the youth of today about the problems of sex, about their problems at home with their parents, about their cheating in school, and other things that are real and vital to them. Unless we can regain a spirit of rapport with these Christian youth, they will not hear us when we speak about God's call and when we preach about how to find the will of God.

Challenge of Missions

Thirdly, *we must present the challenge of the mission fields and other service opportunities.* I doubt seriously that God can effectively lay upon the heart of a young person in our church that he ought to be a medical missionary or a teacher or a nurse, or a pastor or an evangelist in Brazil, or in Nigeria, or in greater New York, or the Los Angeles area, or some other great mission field if *that one has never been exposed* to the challenge, the need, the particular knowledge and information that is available about that particular mission field. I believe that our teaching and our preaching ought to be more saturated with the dissemination of information.

That is why I try to use a missionary in my church every time one is available. A firsthand testimony, a firsthand experience shared with young people about what the mission field is, what its challenges are, what its needs are, and who the people are who are there, contributes to the atmosphere of calling out the called. We ought to take advantage of every opportunity to dramatically present modern missions to our youth. The adults may be challenged to give their money, but the youth will give their lives!

Dr. Baker James Cauthen, the executive secretary of our Foreign Mission Board, years ago in his pastorate, used to challenge his people to respond to the call to the mission fields of the world. It is reported that time and time again,

Dr. Cauthen would say (in effect), why don't you go? Why don't you go to this field or that field or some other particular area of the world that he had enumerated? Why don't you answer God's call? Why do you not surrender to foreign missions? Why don't *you* go, he said time and time again, until one day God said to him, why don't *you* go? And he went! Perhaps one reason why we are unwilling to present the challenge of the mission fields and other service opportunities in more detail is that we know that not only will our youth be challenged, but we might be challenged by it and we might have to go!

Value of Prayer

Fourth, *we need to pray the Lord of the harvest that he will send forth laborers into the harvest.* Matthew 9:35-38 teaches this fact clearly. In verse 35 we see *what Jesus did,* his threefold ministry of preaching, teaching, and healing. In verse 36 we see *what Jesus saw.* He saw the multitudes. And we see *what Jesus felt.* He was moved with compassion. Now that is a translation of one word in the original language, *splagnizomai,* which means to have an emotional and physical upheaval on the inside. To translate it into colloquial language, it would be something like this: Jesus, when he saw the multitudes, was sick to his stomach. He was so upset he had a physical and emotional upheaval on the inside, and it is translated, "He was moved with compassion." He suffered with the people. Why? Because he saw them as sheep without a shepherd, harassed and helpless.

In verse 37 we are told *what he (Jesus) said.* "Then saith he unto his disciples, The harvest truly is plentious, but the labourers are few." The problem is not with the prospects. There are plenty of prospects. The problem is not the lost sheep. There are plenty of them. The problem is not the material. The problem is not the message. The problem is not the Word of God. The problem is not the remedy. The problem is not insufficient grace. The one great problem, the one great bottleneck in Jesus' day and in our day is *too few laborers!* That is the problem. Calling out the called, therefore, is the imperative need of the hour.

Then in verse 38 we are told what *Jesus told us to do.* This is what he told his disciples and what he told us to do. He said that the one solution, the one thing to do, the way to call out the called, the way to deal with the problem of too few laborers, is *to pray.* "Pray ye therefore the Lord of the harvest, that he will send forth labourers into his harvest." Send forth" is a mild translation of a strong word, *ekballo,* which literally means throw out from. Jesus said the solution to the problem of too few laborers is to pray the Lord of the harvest that he will throw out, cast out, laborers into the harvest. That is the basic solution to the problem of too few workers in special church-related vocational service. The answer is to pray for God to throw out more laborers and more workers.

The next word in chapter 10 says (connecting it with what has gone before), "And when he [Jesus] had called unto him his twelve disciples, he gave them power," and their names are listed in verse 5. These twelve Jesus sent forth and commanded them to preach, in verse 7, and heal the sick and cleanse the lepers, and raise the dead and cast out demons. Freely you have received, freely give. What is the meaning of it?

The meaning is this. Jesus went about healing, and preaching, and teaching. And he saw the multitudes. He was sick to his stomach. He had a great physical and emotional upheaval because he saw them harassed and helpless as sheep without a shepherd, and he said to his disciples, the problem is not the lost sheep, the problem is not the harvest, the problem is not the sheaves, the problem is too few laborers. The solution: Pray that the Lord of the harvest will throw out laborers into the harvest, and then those whom he commanded to pray like that, *those he himself sent forth* into the harvest, and said, "Preach as ye go."

We had best not become concerned about the shortage of workers, and we had best not become burdened in intercessory prayer in praying for the Lord of the harvest to cast out more workers into the harvest, *unless we ourselves are prepared to be sent forth!* God may send *you* or *me* into the harvest from the comfortable pastorate and the luxurious surroundings that most of us now enjoy in the midst of this affluent society, as we challenge our youth and our congregations. As we pray to God to throw out laborers, God may in turn throw us out into the pioneer fields of this world, on the cutting edge of evangelism and missions in the world today!

Summary

What have I been trying to say? In summary, God has a will for every life. That will is always best, even in changing circumstances.

For instance, a young girl in her teens may commit her life for special mission service and feel definitely that God has called her. Then along comes a young man, and she marries him the first time she is asked. Suddenly her plan, God's plan for her life, is thwarted. She no longer has a sense of call and her mission field opportunities are eliminated by the confinements and responsibilities of marriage and the home. She may have missed her opportunity for the full and perfect initial will of God for her life. But you see, God has a will and a plan for her life even in those extenuating circumstances. And I believe part of our responsibility is to help these not-so-young people who once felt so close to God and understood his will to ascertain what God's will is *now* for them in the circumstances in which they find themselves.

God has a plan for every life. That plan is always best, but that plan and that will, in my opinion, is learned most frequently by a growing, continuing experience of daily encounter with Jesus Christ, always interpreting God's will, not on the basis of some past experience exclusively, but upon the basis of a daily walk and a daily fellowship. It involves asking ever anew, and finding anew the answer to the question, "What would God have me to do today? What is God's will for my life now?"

Only by thus leading our youth and our congregation can we create an atmosphere conducive to calling out the called. God help us to cease ignoring the ever present problem of increasing numbers of youth, and challenge them to nothing less than complete commitment to the lordship of Jesus Christ. This is youth's greatest need, and to this challenge youth will respond.

VIII

The Old Nemesis, Time

Man cannot possess time. It is one thing that is impossible to contain. One never has more than the split second called *now*. Time is an enigma. It cannot be completely comprehended or explained. Some believe that somehow time is involved in the fall of man. Whether or not this is accurate, it points up the fact that time presents its problems. God is obviously not limited by time but man is, and this includes preachers.

God sees yesterday, today, and tomorrow as one and the same time, but the vision of the minister is greatly limited by the time factor. He cannot possibly see what the future holds, nor adequately interpret all of the events of the past or present. He is going in one direction while time is going in another. The plague of modern ministers is *not enough time!* At least we have convinced ourselves that this is a major part of the problem of getting things done.

What Is Time?

Of course theologically and historically there is a difference between the Greek and Hebrew ideas of time. The typical Greek thought suggested time as a circle, that is, the repetition of a similar series of events. Thus in this concept of time, eternity and salvation must be something *beyond* the realm of time. Man could be saved only by being extricated out of time.

The Hebrew or biblical idea of time, however, is depicted as a straight line of events. Salvation and revelation occur in a connected manner during the continuous time process. Eternity is conceived from the biblical standpoint as endless time or God's time. Of course, more important than the *length* is the *quality* of eternity. The Christian life is thus depicted in the New Testament as an abundant and full quality of life.

It seems to me that the problem of many modern ministers is that we in a practical sense at least are trying to revive the old Greek idea of time, that is, time as a circle. We certainly do spend our time going around in circles or spinning our wheels! But there has probably not been too much ministerial speculation on the philosophical nature of time. Our problems are far more practical than this!

Perhaps one of the most crucial decisions the preacher will ever make is in regard to the division and use of his time. I have found it quite profitable in talking with young people about church-related vocations to explain exactly *what the minister does* with his time. It is amazing how revealing such a talk can be! Even our most active young people have never realized the versatility of the pastor's training, background, and experience or the diversity of his enterprises. This is not limited, however, to the youth. Some of the most active adults in the average church have little or no adequate conception of how the minister utilizes his time.

The Division of a Minister's Time

Idealistically I have always conceived of the pastor's time (as far as the ministry is concerned) as being divided into roughly three equal divisions. Firstly, one third of his time would be reserved for study, sermon preparation, general reading, preaching, and teaching. Secondly, one third of his time would be spent in visitation, including sick calls, hospital visits, bereavement circumstances, enlistment visitation, witnessing and prospect visitation. Thirdly, one third of his time would be spent in administrative matters and executive responsibilities including promotion, directing the program, staff leadership, bulletin articles, and so forth.

There is another area of importance in the minister's busy schedule which cannot so readily be categorized as to time or function. I refer to the minister's counseling situations. Actually in my personal experience counseling has occupied some of all of these areas. It depends upon *what kind* of counseling (or interview) is involved. For instance, there is a certain amount of counseling time involved in relation to one's preaching and teaching. Doctrinal and biblical questions, as well as practical application to particular circumstances often must be elucidated. Sometimes conviction precipitated as a result of preaching and/or teaching situations lead to counseling appointments with the pastor.

Again, some counseling situations are directly related to the pastor's visitation ministry. This would include personal soul-winning, bereavement counseling and grief work, extended illnesses, including terminal illnesses, and counseling involving a multitude of domestic problems. Or the counseling might be more directly related to the pastor's administrative responsibilities, such as personal problems, personality conflicts, and technical difficulties brought on by the inevitable clashes involving the tremendously busy programs of the various church organizations.

Some ministers would no doubt prefer a fourth division of time exclusively identified for the counseling ministry. In my opinion this much emphasis on counseling in the pastor's schedule should be given only by those few ministers who have adequate training and experience in psychology and pastoral counseling. I personally am not qualified to serve as a professional marriage and family counselor, a vocational guidance expert, or a psychiatrist specializing in emotional illnesses, although frequently called upon (as are most ministers) for these and a multitude of other problems.

Of course this division of time is quite arbitrary, and it is obvious that it would have to be rather flexible. There are times for instance such as in preparation for a week of Bible study or revival services, that the minister would have to spend a greater portion of his time in study and sermon preparation. On the other hand during an intensive campaign such as the Forward Program or the Sunday School Enlargement Campaign he would need to spend far more time on the administrative and promotional side. Such times in the church calendar as evangelistic crusades or a period of time preceded by a lengthy absence from the field might necessitate much more time being spent in visitation of prospects and/or the sick and the bereaved. Amazingly incomplete as this brief division may seem, most of the minister's activities could be categorized under one of these three headings as far as his local church ministry is concerned.

Whether or not someone else would agree with this arbitrary division of the minister's time is immaterial. The important thing is for the minister to have some idea of the division of time in the varied aspects of his own ministry. For instance, one could visit for days and weeks on end in the average metropolitan community and never complete the prospect file! There obviously must be some sense of perspective and priorities in the minister's busy schedule.

Most ministers enjoy one phase of their work more than another. But the real frustration apparently lies not in the dislike by the minister of any particular responsibility or in the pressing demands of one particular segment at any given time, but it is the problem of *maintaining the proper perspective* toward all of these elements. As you may have already detected, perhaps the most appealing of these ministerial responsibilities to me personally is that of study, preaching, and teaching. But the responsibility of visitation, of being the man of God in a time of crisis, of leading some one to personal faith in Christ, and of ministering at the hospitals, for example, has never lost its thrill. Actually it would be much easier for me to study all the time or to visit all the time. The difficult part is going from one to the other. Perhaps most ministers are constructed this way. Yet it provides a great deal of valuable assistance to visualize in one's mind the practical division of his ministerial time and to realize that visitation is as much a part of the minister's life as is studying and preaching, or administration. It obviously takes some of all, regardless of the individual minister's personal preferences.

Most ministers or at least many ministers today complain of too much administrative involvement, too much promotion, too many mechanics. Of course the Lord has blessed me with an adequate staff. This no doubt adds much that is good to the situation, but I find that administration, promotion, and programing can be as challenging as sermon preparation or prospect visitation. For instance, contrary to the advice of some of my best friends, my study is located in my office at the church, although I maintain a small study at home apart from the rest of the house. My library is not at home, however, except for a few books transported back and forth to the church. My study at home is actually used only at night or on weekends when I would not normally be in the church office. The pastor's study at the church is separated from the hall provided for normal church traffic only by a secretary's office and is easily accessible to any who genuinely desire to see the pastor. Although many fellow ministers have complained of their inability to get any studying done in such a situation as this, to the contrary I have found an inspiration for study coming from the administrative and promotional aspects of the church program. I am glad to have my study adjacent to the other busy offices at the church. This in effect challenges, guides, directs, and inspires me during intensive Bible study and sermon preparation.

Obviously this situation would not be best for every minister. But I do think that the real, contributive value of the administrative side of the minister's life has been largely overlooked by ministers today. Instead of deploring so much time-consuming involvement in the promotional aspects of our work, an open-minded and learning attitude just might reveal some remarkable insights that could be developed into stimulating homiletical material.

Of course much of this can be attributed to the power of concentration. No minister worth his salt can afford not to learn how to study. Most of us learned this in high school, college, or seminary, but unfortunately some ministers have never learned it. It is a fatal error. Although each man must learn to study for himself, it should be obvious that study is primarily a matter of concentration.

Happy indeed is the minister who in *any* circumstances can learn to concentrate on the matter at hand. The self-discipline which produces intense concentration can provide the minister with literally hours of additional study time per week that he would not otherwise have had if he insists on waiting until such time as the ideal circumstances can be maintained for such study. If the student can discipline himself to concentrate on his lessons in the library at school with all the confusion, interruptions, and noise about him, the minister ought to be able to learn to concentrate in the midst of less than ideal surroundings. Most of our frustrations in being able to get anything done in the church office may be attributable to a lack of self-discipline, especially in regard to forced concentration on the matters at hand.

It is extremely unfortunate that our colleges and seminaries (especially Baptist institutions) do not offer courses in methods of study or learning how to study. It seems there is far greater emphasis today on speed-reading courses than on the power and value of concentration. Although the rapid reader might have a distinct advantage over the slower reader when it comes to the periodicals, daily papers, current literature, and general reading, I doubt that anything less than deliberate, slow-of-pace concentration would suffice for Calvin's *Institutes,* Augustine's *Confessions,* or Barth's *Dogmatics.*

In short it seems to me that more important than the *amount* that is read is the *absorption* of what is read, and this comes about only through concentration. If concentration is developed to a sharp razor edge, then time, place, and circumstances will be of little significance. Of course, every study needs a door that can be shut, and every pastor's secretary needs to cultivate the fine art of gracefully saying no, but all else notwithstanding, there is no substitute for the minister himself mastering the self-discipline necessary for concentrated study.

Other Roles of the Minister

Of course the pastor is not always functioning in the role of the minister. He is usually a father, a husband, a citizen of the community, a neighbor, a yardman, engaged in many nonchurch-related responsibilities. The cry today is heard continuously for the pastor to take more time to spend with his family, but *how* the minister spends his time with his family is more important than *how much time* alone. What the minister does with the time he has with his family, what his attitude is toward the members of his family, and how the members of the family react towards the pastor's time with them and away from them are the important things.

It is my firm conviction there are just as many ministers who spend *too much* time with their families as there are who do not spend enough. From experience I have learned that my children, no matter how much time I spend with them, will always demand more. There must, therefore, always be something of an arbitrary decision on my part as to how much time can reasonably be spent with one's family in recreational activities and wholesome study and exploration together, and that this problem must be carefully explained to one's family and especially the children. Perhaps some time could be profitably expended in a genuine discussion among the family members about the problems and opportunities of the wise use of "Daddy's" time. Members of the minister's family must be taught a natural respect for the persistent invasion of family privacy by the various demands of the ministerial position.

Now, I love my family very dearly, and my wife deserves most of the credit for whatever I have achieved as a minister and servant of the Lord. I have learned much from my children, and I have a deep indebtedness to my parents, but Jesus said a man must be willing to leave his family, even his loved ones, those closest to him on earth to serve Christ. Let us not lose sight of this fact as we evaluate the time responsibilities in the minister's busy life. A minister's family relationships must be placed in their proper perspective in the overall spectrum of devotion to Christ and priorities of time and service.

I have also become convinced in recent years that many ministers waste much time in what a schoolteacher used to call "busy work." They spend long hours, perform many tasks, stay on the job, but really never accomplish anything worthwhile. It is amazing how we can spend so much time in doing nothing! Most of us are aware of those paragons of virtue, who arrive at the church office early in the mornings, grab a sandwich for lunch, and frequently burn the midnight oil (at the church, of course). But the acid test is, *what are they doing,* what has been accomplished, are they just clocking time, what are the overall beneficial results of such tenacity?

The minister's philosophy ought to include something of the following: "See how much I can get done today!" As indicated previously right activities are an essential ingredient in mental and spiritual health. A sense of accomplishment must be involved if the minister is to maintain his spiritual equilibrium. No matter how busy we are, if we cannot occasionally point to something that has been accomplished, that has been done, that is finished that is good within itself, then we are foredoomed to failure!

The old nemesis time is every day with us and always will be. As trite as it may seem, we all have the same amount of time, the only difference is what we do with it. Why do some people seem to get so much more out of their time and get so much more accomplished with their time? At least part of the answer is found in purposeful planning, useful execution, and thoughtful reflection on the division and use of the pastor's time.

IX

Pastor-Staff Relationships

Hebrews 11:21 says, "By faith Jacob, when he was a-dying, blessed both the sons of Joseph; and worshipped, leaning upon the top of his staff." Many preachers have jokingly referred to this passage in regard to pastor-staff relationships. It is sometimes considered fatal for a pastor to lean on his staff with the result that like Jacob, he died!

This is certainly not my personal testimony. I am thoroughly convinced that to a great degree I am what I am today as a minister of the gospel and especially as pastor of First Baptist Church, Dothan, because of the members of my staff. These dedicated Christian men and women have the same sense of calling and destiny as I. They have a loyalty to the pastor and church, a dedication to Christ and a genuine, non-maudlin spirituality that is amazing to behold!

No pastor worth his salt could possibly fail to recognize, especially when involved in a large church in the twentieth century, that he cannot do an effective job as promoter and administrator without the assistance of an adequate staff. There is no blessedness in isolationism, as a nation, as a church or as an individual pastor. We are all interdependent.

We are in this work together. We are co-laborers together with Christ. I love and respect each member of my staff and unless I am greatly deceived I have the love and respect reciprocally of them.

First Among Equals

My basic philosophy of pastor-staff relationships begins with the premise that the pastor is first among equals. It is obvious that God calls men and women to be ministers of education, ministers of music, ministers of visitation, youth directors, staff evangelists, even church secretaries, kitchen hostesses, building superintendents, and so forth. Nevertheless, every family needs a daddy. Every organization needs a head. And I am firmly committed to the idea that the pastor must be first among equals, the administrative and organizational head of the church staff, if the church organization is to function smoothly.

This, of course, does not forego the availability of freedom, initiative, and creativity on the part of the staff members. As long as the staff members understand their relationship to the pastor and agree to this in advance there will be no problems in this regard. In fact in all of my ministry I can never recall having had to invoke administrative authority over any other staff member since we had had a clear understanding about the relationship from the beginning. Cooperation, fellowship, partnership, and service are the key words in pastor-staff relationships.

It is true in my church and many others that the congregation extends a formal call to all staff members upon recommendation of the staff committee. This does not mean, however, that each staff member is responsible only to and directly to the church congregation and/or staff committee. Actually the staff members (at least the ministerial staff members) in my church are responsible directly to the pastor. Their respective secretaries are responsible to them with the minister of education having general supervision of the business offices and organizational activities of the church. Within the area of each staff member's job description and understanding of his work there is room for plenty of creative thinking, implementation of ideas, and program innovations without any interference from the pastor. But all of the staff members clearly understand that in the case of a dispute, a misunderstanding, a serious difference of opinion, or a question of program priorities, that the final decision would be made by the administrative leader, who in this church is the pastor.

Personally I cannot conceive of a church functioning properly with several heads instead of one. I do not mean to question the validity of this theory as believed in and practiced (apparently successfully) in other churches throughout our Convention. But in my own personal experience I know of none where this particular type of responsibility and organization has worked effectively. Let those who propagate such a theory of church oganization and administrative leadership come forward to enumerate specific, successful examples of multiheaded and group-directed church programs.

Presuppositions for Staff Members

Actually it has been my practice throughout my ministry to interview personally all prospective staff members. During this informal conversation there have been several key points of emphasis and understanding which we have discussed. These qualifications or requirements, however, for staff members are built upon certain basic presuppositions, that is, that the staff member first of all *must be a Christian,* meaning that he has had a personal, vital experience with Jesus Christ as Saviour and Lord. Secondly, he must be a *witness for Christ* and to his Christian faith.

Of course some will indicate that this could be assumed from the beginning for any prospective staff member in a Baptist church. In my opinion this would be a fatal mistake. We cannot assume that a seminary degree is necessarily synonymous with personal salvation, or that a formal education and even ordination is synonymous with effective sharing of one's witness and testimony. I would not for a moment presume to pass judgment on the genuineness of the conversion experience of pastors and staff members throughout our churches in the Southern Baptist Convention. At the same time any person who is considered as a prospective co-laborer in my church must give satisfactory indication that he has experienced the new birth, and that he is willing and unafraid to make a positive effort to share his faith with those who have not yet had that experience. It seems to me that we are in grave danger of assuming too much in this day and age when so many other denominations, and apparently seminaries and so-called Christian colleges, are evidently failing to give proper emphasis to the necessity for personal regeneration and effective personal witnessing.

This is a day and age when soul-winning, personal witnessing, sharing a testimony, and so forth is looked upon as passe and out of date. Even denominational leaders, supposedly leaders in evangelism, of some denominations are now suggesting that what we have been taught in the way of personal witnessing and soul-winning in the past is really nothing more than proselyting. And this is no longer considered in vogue or ethical for modern day church members. What a tragedy, we say. But in the light of what is happening should we not as ministers of the gospel do our very best to insure that only truly born-again, witnessing believers in Christ are employed in staff positions in our churches?

Let me make it clear that I am not expecting out of any staff member what I would not be willing to do myself. The same presuppositions for prospective staff members are applicable to the pastor as well. But I also strive to make it definitely clear to any prospective staff member that I expect him or her to be a Christian, to act like a Christian, and witness for Christ as a regular part of his Christian commitment. All of this is made clear before and in advance of any discussion of job description or specific areas of responsibilities. This I believe we have the right to expect and to be assured of as far as any future co-laborer is concerned.

Requirements for Staff Members

Based upon these two presuppositions are the following three requirements for staff members in my church.

(1) There must be *unquestionable loyalty* to the pastor and the total church program. If a prospective staff member cannot work with, and cooperate with the present pastor and present church program and organization, then he does not need to consider joining such an organization. If he cannot work as a member of the team, then he should not join the team. I want it clearly understood from the beginning that a staff member who finds that at any time in the course of his tenure of service that he can no longer work with, or cooperate, or morally support the pastor and the church program, that the pastor should be first to know, and that he

(the staff member) should feel the responsibility for making a change. There might be some difference in relationship here in a situation where the pastor was called to a church that was already fully staffed. Most of us have not had this experience and usually the pastor has the responsibility as well as opportunity of selecting his own staff members.

No pastor can operate efficiently and minister effectively if he does not have an atmosphere of mutual trust and respect with his staff. The pastor must not only feel that he is trusted by the staff members, but he must have a sense of security built upon trust in the staff members, especially when he is away from the field. Chaos is the inevitable result of mistrust and suspicion within the ministerial and staff circle in the local church.

(2) A staff member must demonstrate and maintain the *ability to work with people.* It does not matter how loyal to the pastor and the church program an individual may be or how adept at performing his various tasks, if he cannot get along with the people in the church, if he cannot work with them and love them, and be patient with them, in spite of their immaturity or lack of Christian attitudes in certain areas, then he cannot function effectively on the church staff. I have seen men fail in this particular point, men who were skilled and dedicated to their task, who loved their pastor and the church, but simply had no ability to cooperate in the give-and-take of everyday responsibilities. We are working with people and unless we can get along with them our work will be unsuccessful.

(3) Finally there must be acceptable *performance of the assigned tasks.* It is not enough for a staff member to be able to get along with people, have a scintillating personality, and demonstrate faithfulness and dependability to the church

and pastor. He must also be able to perform his particular responsibilities with dispatch and efficiency. If he is a music director he must be able to direct music; if he is a staff evangelist he must be able to cultivate prospects and visit constantly; if he is a minister of education he must be able to direct the educational program; if he is a youth director he must be able to guide the youth program. This requirement ought to be obvious, but unfortunately many seem to accept positions of responsibility with little or no commitment to the main task at hand. A discussion in advance of the call to any staff member of these three areas based on these presuppositions has in my opinion contributed immeasurably to a tremendous rapport, camaraderie, and healthy relationship between myself as pastor and those godly men and women with whom I have labored during these years of ministry.

The Job Description

Another thing which needs to be discussed in advance of the employment of a staff member is what has come to be called the job description. Some churches insist on spelling out lengthy and detailed job descriptions even in the constitution and bylaws of the church. Such inflexibility creates more problems than it resolves. In fact since being pastor of First Baptist Church, Dothan, I have learned that it is a good idea to have a rather flexible job description when the staff committee sets out initially seeking to fill a vacancy on the staff. After all we ought to be interested first in calling God's man or woman to the particular position, and we ought to be honest enough to face up to the fact that no one person can do everything well. At least no one person can do *everything* as well as he can do *some* things.

Of course there must be a general job description in mind, and this is rather clearly defined by whatever position is vacant at the time or whatever position is about to be created. The main thing ought to be the *seeking of the right person, God's person, a spiritual person, a qualified person,* and fitting the details of the job description to that person's forte, strong point, area of greatest effectiveness. Why should we hamstring staff members by molding them into the church's conception or the pastor's conception of what the particular position ought to be when his or her strong points may be in another direction? Far better would it be to capitalize on a qualified person's strong points than to unnaturally attempt to force him to conform to a preconceived mold that may be only theoretically conceived in the first place.

For instance, it is possible to have a minister of music whose ministry and work may be entirely different from that of another minister of music. This is true also for the minister of education. Actually this has been true in my experience at First Baptist Church, Dothan. We have now a minister of music whose major emphasis is on the graded choir program and choir enlistment, although his predecessor's emphasis was on special music, solos, special choir features and presentations. At the time when this person came to our staff there was a great need for this latter type of emphasis, with our television and radio ministry, and the image of our church was greatly enhanced in the community because of the contribution this man made. Now, however, other needs are being met through an elaborate choir and Music Ministry affecting many lives throughout our entire church and community.

The two ministers of education that have served with me in Dothan have been men of completely different abilities, experiences, and interests. One was primarily an associate pastor, since he had served several pastorates capably and efficiently. The present staff member in this position, although having served elsewhere as associate pastor, is primarily an educational director, an organizational man, and a writer. Both are well-trained, well-qualified men, but with varying interests, abilities, and experiences. Either one of them would be greatly handicapped if he were suddenly forced into the mold of the other. Yet both have served faithfully and efficiently in the office of minister of education in the same church, the one succeeding the other in that office.

Such differences in job descriptions for the same positions are obvious in other areas as well. The youth program is an example. Some churches call youth directors who are recreational directors, who are activities-oriented, whereas in our church the youth director is actually a minister of education specializing in youth, and most of the programing is done through the established organizations of the church. This particular person has a seminary degree and agrees that there is little or no room in our present situation for an extensive recreational activities program, which would be in direct competition with several other well developed programs in our community.

Staff members have varying talents and personalities just as pastors do. It is far better (in my opinion) to extend the call with a clear understanding that the staff members will be free within the general area of a broad job description to develop their talents and personalities in a creative way. That way they will have freedom as well as responsibilities. Thus they will be happier, they will tend to stay longer, and they will make more beneficial, spiritual contributions to the lives of our church members than would be possible otherwise.

Social Relationships

Perhaps a word needs to be said about the personal relationships between the pastor and staff members including the families involved. Although I feel that I have been a close personal friend to most of my staff members, there is actually very little social life or family relationships between the pastor and family and most of the staff members and their families. This is, of course, necessitated in part by the limitations of time. There is something deeper here than this, however. Those of us who work together all day and all week and even on Sundays, perhaps need to withdraw from each other, especially during the informal times of recreation and social activities.

This is not to say that there cannot be and should not be times of fellowship and informal activities involving the staff members and their families. We have had regular periods of social activities for years, but it is still true that over-familiarity breeds contempt, and just as every pastor knows, his appreciation and love for his church often is enhanced after being off the field for a week or two. So our appreciation, love, and respect for fellow staff members is enhanced by not feeling obligated to spend all of our social and recreational hours together.

In conclusion let it be said that no pastor of a large church can succeed without the cooperation, understanding, and dedication of the staff members. Each church is organized differently. Some will find it necessary to have certain staff positions that would be entirely superfluous in other situations. My particular church presently has the following positions: minister of education, minister of music, youth director, mission pastor, staff evangelist, kitchen hostess, maintenance superintendent, pastor's secretary, educational secretary, financial secretary, music secretary, records and visitation secretary, receptionist, church visitor, and several janitors and maids. At least three or four of these positions have been created during this pastorate. Several job descriptions have been rewritten and titles changed.

At best this particular organization is quite flexible and is susceptible to change as soon as it becomes apparent that some other position or organization will get the job done more effectively. Each church must make its own decisions, but only the pastor can create the atmosphere in which a healthy and understanding relationship with his staff members can be permanently established. In fact I must quite frankly state that most of the responsibility for creating this kind of healthy atmosphere rests squarely upon the shoulders of the pastor. My observation indicates that most examples of deteriorated pastor-staff relationships were precipitated initially by an overbearing pastoral authority, a completely withdrawn attitude on the part of the pastor, or more frequently a simple failure to clarify the relationship from the beginning.

X

Christ Loved the Church

Varied indeed are the modern definitions of the nature and function of the church. No book on the ministry would be complete without adequately confronting the challenges to the church as an effective instrument of God in the world today. The church today is being identified as a social agency, a political forum, an economic sounding board, a civic club or a fraternal organization, just to mention a few things. There are those who are outwardly saying the church as an organization has served its usefulness; it is now outdated and thus outmoded, and subsequently foredoomed to failure.

This present-day ridicule of the church is to me something on the order of smearing the reputation of my wife! The very idea of such a thing! My wife's faithfulness is above and beyond debate as far as her husband is concerned. And the distinctive usefulness and value of the church in today's world is also beyond question! Despite the fact that it may be considered in vogue to criticize the effectiveness of the church in the modern world, I am thoroughly convinced that what is needed more than ever is a recapturing of the strategic role and ministry of the New Testament church.

This present age needs *more* not *less* of the church of Jesus Christ!

The church has always enjoyed a unique and significant role in my life. Our family was a truly church-going family: Sunday morning, Sunday evening, and Wednesday night. There was no distinction made between Sunday School and morning worship, or between Training Union and evening worship! We went when the first activity began and stayed until everything was over. The same was true for revivals, study courses, and special events.

There was never any debate in our home as to whether or not certain services would be attended. When the hour came, we were present in God's house in the company of other faithful believers. Absence indicated only one thing: some providential hindrance, such as sickness, death in the family, or job necessity. I thank God for this early discipline and training in the cultivation of good church attendance habits!

The Church in the New Testament

My favorite passage of Scripture regarding the church is Ephesians 5:25, which says, "Christ also loved the church, and gave himself for it." Whenever anyone begins to deprecate the church or make light of its value today I usually respond by quoting this passage. After all if Jesus Christ loved the church enough to die for it, then we ought to love it enough to support it and if necessary defend it! No matter what may be wrong with the church and its program today, Christ loved it and died for it, and that is justification enough for me to give the church unqualified support.

The founder of the church is, of course, Jesus Christ, who said, "I will build my church" (Matt. 16:18). Thus the church is a fellowship of believers who are literally *owned* bv

Jesus Christ. It is also called the church of God, which he purchased with his own blood (Acts 20:28). The church is further referred to as the church of the living God and the pillar and ground of truth (1 Tim. 3:15). Moreover the church is the body of which Christ is the head (Col. 1:18,24).

Of course, it has frequently been pointed out that there are only two references to the church by name in the Gospel accounts of the recorded teachings of Jesus, both occurring in Matthew (16:18;18:17). Yet competent scholars (such as R. Newton Flew in his *Jesus and His Church*) have adequately documented the theory that the church *in its embryonic form* is quite definitely present throughout the earthly ministry of our Lord. The four great withdrawals of Jesus with his disciples, for example, enunciated in A. T. Robertson's *Harmony of the Gospels*, is an illustration of the early beginnings of the church as an instrument of worship and instruction. Furthermore there is no real question but that the church as an institution as well as a living organism is paramount throughout the remaining portions of the New Testament.

I love the church. It has always been difficult to understand how some ministers maintain such a negative attitude toward the church. Unless one is to fulfil the role of an ancient prophet in modern times, he must be (at least to a certain degree) dependent upon a church for not only material support but for an opportunity to declare his message as well. God has called us to preach, but he has also called us to be the pastor of a church, and this is important also.

The Doctrine of the Church

My basic optimistic view of the church as an effective instrument of God in the world today is built also upon the

New Testament concept of what the church is and what it does. First of all, *what the church is* in the New Testament is described primarily in two words, *ecclesia* and *koinonia.* The word *ecclesia* always means an assembly of people in the New Testament, never a building. This word in the Old Testament background means congregation or assembly, and it is used of a local assembly in Acts 19:41. In addition there seem to be three different uses of *ecclesia* in the New Testament: (1) a local Christian community, (2) a number of such local communities, and (3) all the redeemed in Christ.

The *ecclesia* is considered as the messianic community in the New Testament, a new Israel. The very same words found in the Old Testament to describe the nation of Israel are found in the New Testament to describe the church. A casual reading of Exodus 19:5-6 and 1 Peter 2:9-10 will readily illustrate this point. The church originated in the redemptive act of God in Christ. Other assemblies originated through the volition of man, but this is an assembly of God's called-out ones. The *ecclesia* is an assembly of those who have been called of God unto everlasting and abundant life.

Koinonia is also a descriptive word of what the church is, according to the New Testament. The word means participation in something in which others are also participating. It connotes an active sharing with others who are sharing in the same enterprise. In the Christian context *koinonia* means a sharing together by Christians in Jesus Christ and his spiritual benefits.

The church involves us in a twofold relationship, one vertical and the other horizontal. We are in right relationship with God *vertically* because of our faith in God's redemptive work in Christ. But this automatically involves us in a relationship with other believers in the church. This is the *horizontal* relationship of love for the brethren. Jesus taught us in Matthew 18 that this fellowship within the church should display the qualities of humility, responsibility, self-renunciation, care for the individual, discipline, and forgiveness. If there is one thing clear in the teaching of Jesus it is simply this: one cannot be in right relationship with God if he is in constant wrong relationship with his fellowmen, especially those who are within the church! Our relationship to others, particularly other believers, definitely is a reflection of our true relationship to the Heavenly Father.

The practical application of this is demonstrated in bearing one another's burdens, in weeping with those who weep, and rejoicing with those who rejoice. Every Christian is responsible for himself and for others as well. Incidentally, William Barclay points out that it is often easier to weep with those fellow-believers who weep than it is to rejoice with those who rejoice! It is not too difficult to display genuine Christian sympathy to another in a trying, bereavement circumstance. But it may be very difficult to genuinely rejoice and thank God for the great success of another person! We preachers are particularly vulnerable at this point.

In summary the church is the *temple of God* (2 Cor. 6:16; 1 Cor. 3:16) and the *people of God* (1 Peter 2:10). The church is also the *body of Christ* (Eph. 5:21–23; Rev. 19:7–9;21:9). These are figures used in the New Testament to identify and define the nature of the church.

Secondly, *what the church does* is described in the New Testament also in two words, *kerygma* and *didache*. The word *kerygma* means proclamation or the thing preached. It meant in New Testament times primarily the telling of the good news to people who had not heard it before, rather than our type preaching today. The substance of this *kerygma* consisted particularly in the message of the cross and the resurrection of Jesus, especially as originally prophesied in the Old Testament Scriptures and fulfilled in the life and death of the Nazarene. The *kerygma* always included the call to repentance and faith in Jesus Christ.

The *didache* (teaching), on the other hand, meant ethical instruction, instruction in the faith, theological exposition or apologetics. The New Testament makes a clear distinction between preaching (*kerygma*) and teaching (*didache*). The *kerygma* was primarily the public proclamation of Christ to the unregenerate, whereas *didache* or ethical instruction followed and was based upon the essential Christian message of what God had done in Jesus Christ.

To put it in modern language the basic twofold purpose of the church is to win the lost to Christ and build up the saved in the faith. These are the functions of worship and evangelism. The essential items of education, training, and ministry are inherently involved in a proper understanding of New Testament worship and evangelism. There can be no true worship or evangelism that does not involve (at least to some degree) education, training, and ministry. They are definitely interrelated in the New Testament. There is no justification for the continuing existence of the church in today's world apart from its continued commitment to the biblical concept of what the church is to be and what it is to do.

The Practical Side

Yes, some are saying we no longer need the church, that we are now in the post-Protestant era. And it may well be true that if the church as we know it is to survive it must radically alter its program of work. *But I am committed unequivocally to the institution of the church as the living organism Christ, its founder, intended it to be!* It is the Lord's church, divine in origin, founded and built by Jesus Christ with the assurance of eternal significance and victory. It is no losing cause with which we are thus involved.

Many rebellious youth today are saying they can accept Jesus but not his church, especially as presently organized and functioning. Yet there must be a practical side to the divine organism. There must be some kind of organization if the organism is to function and minister. No minister who has realistically confronted the problems in regard to the church and the world today would dare suggest the church is ideally all it should be or what Christ intended. Yet the failure to achieve perfection does not invalidate our efforts to be the people of God in our generation.

Of course, the human side of the church is just exactly that, *human* with all the failures, shortcomings, and frailties appertaining thereto. Therefore the church as an organization will always have its frustrations and to a certain extent its ineffectiveness because sinful human beings are its ministers, leaders, and members! Yet this should not unduly alarm us, and definitely should not be used as a rationalism to exclude us from active participation and support of the local church.

Actually the rebellious, nonauthoritarian critics of the church have *no better alternative* to present. It is relatively easy to be an iconoclast rather than a participant in God's redemptive plan. So many today are tearing down, but seemingly few are trying to build up. It is true that individuals have the right of criticism and honest questioning of the role and function of the modern church. But *it is also true that criticism carries with it the inherent responsibility to contribute something positive and good to the whole!* Too many are willing only to pronounce judgment without the concomitant responsibility associated therewith.

The desperate need is for strong, committed leadership to stand up and issue the challenge to unselfish service for the cause of Christ through the church! I am thoroughly convinced that many of the critics of the church would not have nearly as much ammunition if some of us on the inside did not furnish them so much! The need in this regard now is for church leaders to turn from the negative to the positive as far as the church is concerned. If the leadership is permanently disillusioned, the followers will be likewise infected.

The time has come to close ranks. The church is not all it should be, or all it must become. But by the grace of God (and the cooperation of the redeemed of God, especially the ministers and leaders) the church will continue to be an effective arm of the Lord in the midst of a crooked and perverse generation. There is hope; it is not too late. The church *is* relevant *and* necessary. We simply need to return to the New Testament teachings concerning what a church is to be and to do. There can be no substitute for strong, optimistic, forward-looking, and relevant leadership for the church of Jesus Christ in our day. Remember: Christ loved the church and gave himself for it!

Bibliography

De Dietrich, Suzanne. *The Witnessing Community.* Philadelphia: Westminster, 1958.

Dodd, C. H. *The Apostolic Preaching and Its Developments.* London: Hodder and Stoughton, 1936.

FLEW, R. NEWTON. *Jesus and His Church.* Second edition; London: Epworth, 1943.

McCALL, DUKE K. *What Is the Church?* Nashville: Broadman, 1958.

NELSON, J. ROBERT. *The Realm of Redemption.* Greenwich, Conn.: Seabury, 1951.

RICHARDSON, ALAN. *A Theological Word Book of the Bible.* New York: Macmillan, 1950.

TRUEBLOOD, ELTON. *The Company of the Committed.* New York: Harper, 1961.

XI

Breaking Out Stained-Glass Windows

A rash of shooting out plate-glass windows in our community recently was reported in the press. Both store fronts and church buildings were the victims. A variety of air rifles, pellet guns, and pistols had apparently been used. No explanation other than sheer vandalism was indicated.

There is a spiritual analogy in these incidents, however, that could be beneficial for our churches. The churches themselves need to break out of the enclosed edifices within which we have too long confined ourselves. We need to break out of the four walls and stained glass of the church buildings and literally get out into the world where the people are and the needs are great! As has been indicated by others we need to get the church on the outside where it has room to breathe; we need to carry the message into the marketplaces of human life, to get out of the cathedrals just as the early churches got out of the synagogues. The greatest heresy of the modern church may after all be the building itself!

Outside the Walls

Actually, real and effective worship can be best measured by what happens outside the walls of the sanctuary, after the actual worship services have been concluded. The New Testament churches met together for worship and fellowship but then disseminated themselves into the everyday world for service. Today we have in effect reversed the process. We attempt to bring the world into the church building in order to evangelize the unregenerate, when the New Testament pattern indicates that evangelism was done not primarily when the church was *gathered* but when it was *scattered* into the byways and hedges.

Elton Trueblood's concept of the church as a company of committed Christians is apropos at this point. The church ought to be a spiritual filling station for the redeemed to be refueled and then go out for ministry and service. All the saints are to be equipped for the work of the ministry according to the best translation of Ephesians 4:11-13.

There is a new day of emphasis upon ministering, especially among Southern Baptists. "Mission Action" has become a familiar term. The social *implications* of the gospel have now become *responsibilities* and *imperatives* and rightly so. The biblical foundation for such literal involvement in ministering to the total needs of all men under the lordship of Christ is apparent. "Unto the least of these, my brethren" has become a challenging reality in practical service for many.

Of course the church is to be a redeemed and a redeeming society. The gospel of individual, personal redemption in Christ *is* the gospel of societal involvement and redemption. It is indeed a false dichotomy which distinguishes between the two. Nevertheless Jesus resisted the temptation consistently to minister exclusively to the physical needs of humanity. He was always concerned with the total needs which included man's spiritual relationship to God. The church of today must ever do the same.

The Poor and Needy

Although there are many areas of need where the church must become involved, I would like to explore in some detail one of those specific areas, namely that of our ministry to the needy and the poor. This involves, of course, the Christian philosophy of labor, and the apostle Paul speaks directly to this matter.

In 2 Thessalonians 3:6-15 Paul writes, "Now we command you, brethren, in the name of our Lord Jesus Christ, that ye withdraw yourselves from every brother that walketh disorderly, and not after the tradition which he received of us. For yourselves know how ye ought to follow us: for we behaved not ourselves disorderly among you; neither did we eat any man's bread for nought; but wrought with labour and travail night and day, that we might not be chargeable to any of you: not because we have not power, but to make ourselves an ensample unto you to follow us. For even when we were with you, this we commanded you, that if any would not work, neither should he eat. For we hear that there are some which walk among you disorderly, working not at all, but are busybodies. Now them that are such we command and exhort by our Lord Jesus Christ, that with quietness they work, and eat their own bread. But ye, brethren, be not weary in well-doing. And if any man obey not our word by this epistle, note that man, and have no company with him, that he may be ashamed. Yet count him not as an enemy, but admonish him as a brother."

Strange words indeed are these when they fall on modern ecclesiastical ears. These are words relevant to church discipline, an almost lost concept in this modern age. Unquestionably it is a concept that has been abused by the church in certain periods of its history but one which is almost completely overlooked and neglected today.

When Paul says withdraw yourselves from such disorderly ones he means withdraw in fellowship, withdraw in the agape meal or the love feast, the fellowship supper, and withdraw in the observance of the Lord's Supper. It was a method of exercising church discipline responsibly. And it is these words that are quite strange to modern ears as I have indicated. Are we failing today to live up to the implications of what Paul says?

Yet this teaching concerning church discipline by the apostle is in the context of a labor problem. There was a situation that had developed as a result of misunderstanding the implication of a particular teaching of the apostle when he was present in the church at Thessalonica (as well as in the first letter to the Thessalonians) that had resulted in a group who refused to work but depended upon the generosity and charity of the remaining portions of the Christian community for their daily subsistence. Here we see the apostle emphasizing his agreement with the basic biblical concept beginning with the Old Testament from the day of creation when God worked, to the dignity, the sanctity, the majesty of honest labor and of hard work. Now it is in this context of expressing his views on labor and hard work that the matter of church discipline arises.

Let us examine this passage under a threefold heading. First of all, the *circumstances* under which Paul expressed his philosophy of labor; secondly, the *statement* of his philosophy itself; and finally the *justification* for his simple but complex idea.

The Circumstances

The *circumstances* are quite obvious if you carefully read the passage. It was a situation where because of Paul's teaching concerning the second coming of Christ (both by his personal appearance and by the epistle which bears the name, 1 Thessalonians) there were those who had become so enamored with the expectation of the Lord's return they had quit their jobs, they had stopped their daily endeavors, and were literally sitting down awaiting the Lord's return. Paul said this is a false philosophy, a false interpretation of living in the expectation of the Lord's return. In fact I think John Wesley said it aptly when he was asked the question, "Mr. Wesley, if you knew that the Lord would return tomorrow night what would you do?" Wesley replied, "I would go right along fulfilling my appointments on up to the time when he comes. I would like for him to find me working just that way." I believe this is a proper interpretation of the teaching of the apostle concerning living in the light of the expectation of the Lord's return. It is not that we quit our jobs and stop our responsibilities and gaze into the heavens, putting on our white robes to wait the momentary coming of the Lord. But rather the proper way to live in the expectation of the coming of Christ is to be fulfilling our daily responsibilities, just as if we had the assurance that he would not return for a hundred years or for our lifetime.

Paul said in this context that there are those who are walking disorderly among you. Several times he mentions that. In verse 6 he says, "Every brother that walketh disorderly, and not after the manner in which he received of us," and again in verse 11 he says, "There are some which walk among you disorderly." There were problems in the church of Thessalonica. Now he goes on to the next phrase in verse 11 to identify the disorderly. In what way were they disorderly in the church at Thessalonica? "There are some which walk among you disorderly," he said, "working not at all, but are busybodies." Now there is a play on words in the language of the New Testament that is not obvious here in the English translation, but the words are very similar and in fact Paul is saying this: they are *not busy* but *busybodies*. They are not being busy, they are busy being busybodies. They are not working, they are always working around people; their only business is the business of being a busybody.

Now of course we have all heard from our youth that an idle mind is the devil's workshop. I was interested that etymologically the word "idle" does not mean the cessation of all activity, but rather it means the *wrong kind* of activity, such as an idle schoolboy who is busily carving up the desk or pestering his neighbor. Idle has the etymological implication of not just cessation of activity but doing the wrong things.

This in itself is one of the greatest explanations of why idleness is wrong as far as the apostle is concerned. He said they are not busy, they are not doing their work, they are not performing their respective tasks and subsequently, having time on their hands, they begin to interfere in everybody else's business. They are not busy, they are busybodies. Now the apostle mentions this again in the Epistle of 1 Timothy. First Timothy 5:13 says, "And withal they learn to be idle, wandering about from house to house; and not only idle, but tattlers also and busybodies, speaking things which they ought not." An idle mind is indeed the devil's workshop and idleness produces activity in an area where we ought not to be. These people were not busy; they were busybodies. They quit their jobs, they quit tasks, they were not working, and this is a misinterpretation of how to be living in the expectation of the coming again of Christ. Now it is in this context that Paul *states* his philosophy of labor.

In a nutshell it is quite simple. Paul says, "No work, no eats!" And strangely enough that oversimplification (as it would be interpreted today) solved the problem. The labor problem of the Christians in the church at Thessalonica in the first century was solved by a simple philosophy; let these people alone, let them work quietly and eat the fruit produced by the work of their own hands, and if they don't work they don't eat. No longer let them be parasites, and the problem evidently was solved. We never hear about it again in the history of the New Testament church.

Paul's Statement

Paul's philosophy is stated on at least two occasions in this passage "If any would not work, neither should he eat," and "That with quietness they work, and eat their own bread." Therefore if they don't produce their own bread then they don't have anything to eat. A simple philosophy but the meaning of it is this: that every person capable of doing so ought to carry his own weight. It means that we ought to carry our part of the responsibility and eliminate overdependence upon one another and freeloading as a way of life. It means that the basic philosophy of labor from a Christian standpoint is an honest day's wages for an honest day's labor and both aspects are important.

Whether or not we are thrown in the role of doing the work ourselves, an honest day's labor and an honest day's wages based upon the principle of integrity rather than the desire to deceive or the desire to get something for nothing is the basic philosophy for work.

Now this is, of course, as I have indicated, in keeping with the total biblical concept of labor. Labor is sacred. Work has dignity. Honest work, honest labor is always approved in the Christian concept. It is not true as has been erroneously interpreted that labor per se was the result of the fall of man in the Garden of Eden. Rather, the drudgery and the monotony that result from man's dissatisfaction with his God-given responsibility are part of the curse placed upon man because of his fall into sin. And only then after the fall the Word said "in the sweat of thy face shalt thou eat bread." Remember that Adam and Eve were commanded in the Garden of Eden before they ate the forbidden fruit, before the fall of man, and before the curse because of man's sin, to tend the garden. Work was and is an integral part of God's creation and man's responsibility in that creation plan. It is something dignified, majestic, and worthy of our participation.

The Christian concept is that everybody ought to share his own part of the load. There ought not to be any freeloaders on the Christian community or the society as a whole. Now quite obviously excluded from this are invalids, infants, and elderly people too weak to be able to perform any menial tasks. We must not make the mistake, however, of excluding many physically incapacitated from doing certain types of work, who, especially in our society (in fact more so in our modern society than in the New Testament society) can perform these tasks that are available to them. But what it means is that if a person is able to do anything and can do so he ought not depend upon others to do for him what he could do for himself! Every Christian ought to share his responsibility, his part of the load, and hold up his own weight. Paul's simple philosophy is expressed as follows: if men would not work then neither should they eat.

In other words, I interpret this to mean that the basic solution to the remedy for any problem between labor and management today must be built upon the basic integrity of all parties involved and the desire for proper Christian motivation and the absence of this spirit of the "gimmie" philosophy, "What's in it for me? How much can I get out of it?" without any regard for what is fair or equitable for the other party involved. It seems to me this must be our attitude in whatever area of labor we are involved, labor, management, government, unions, or what not, our own business or working for the other man. There must be this basic concept of an honest day's labor for an honest day's wages. If we are doing the labor then we must be willing to give and invest fairly and honestly based upon trust, respect, and integrity before we expect to receive an honest day's wages. If we are, from the standpoint of the employer who pays the wages, negotiating the contract or leading in that regard from a governmental or advisory position, we must be willing to pay equitably a wage in keeping with the spirit of those who are doing the work.

Now let's go a step further in applying this situation to today. I feel that the emphasis on poverty and the poverty programs supported by our government are quite apropos as we interpret this principle from the teachings of Paul in the New Testament. It is very difficult for me to justify the public protestation of apparently able-bodied men and women who exercise pressure upon the government and upon the nation particularly through the national news media to seemingly instigate support for themselves without the acceptance of the compatible responsibilities. It is difficult for me to understand those who demand assistance who are able to work, especially when there are jobs and positions available.

Now this poses a very strange situation. As Christians we are to be compassionate. We must help our brother in need. When we walk down the roadside and see the man who has fallen among thieves we are not to philosophize and ask what was he doing there and whether or not he is worthy of our assistance. That is not the question at all. Jesus never stopped helping somebody to try to ascertain whether they were worthy or not. Jesus just helped them! When he could help them, he helped them. Now they were always unworthy as far as others were concerned. That is why they had not helped them. But it was those considered by society to be unworthy that Jesus helped most! So that isn't the question at all. I *am* my brother's keeper, and my neighbor is *anybody who is in need* regardless of the circumstances or how he got himself there. If he hungers then I must share from the abundance of my table with him. The Christian attitude is one of compassion and the motivation of genuine concern to help people as it is within our means to do so.

So since we as Christians are to be the compassionate ones and the concerned ones this places us in the peculiar circumstance of criticizing on the surface apparently well-meaning, well-planned, well-organized programs for eliminating poverty. It places us in quite a peculiar position to criticize our government when the governmental programs are supposed to be committed to the elimination of the problem of poverty. We are looked at askance when we raise the slightest doubt or question about the supposed propriety of such programs, because we are the ones who are supposed to be automatically interested in the alleviation of the problems of the poor, in the elimination of poverty.

And Christians certainly are interested in that. But if a particular political expedient and a given program tend to degrade the God-given personality of the individuals involved, and to increase and encourage the problem rather than eliminate it, then we have a moral obligation to speak out against it. This is the problem as I understand it in many of the poverty programs in which our government and other organizations are engaged today. It seems to be completely incompatible with the philosophy of the apostle Paul; every person must share his own portion of responsibility, everybody must tote his end of the plank, everybody should work for his subsistence if he is able to work. If our charity and our benevolence is propagating the idea of something for nothing and denying the biblical concept of the dignity of honest labor and honest work, then it is becoming what is called "pauperizing charity" (W. F. Adeney). That is the kind of charity and benevolence that produces poverty, penury, and paupers instead of alleviating those involved in it or extricating ourselves from it entirely in our society.

Paul's Justification

Now we come lastly to the *justification* for Paul's viewpoint. His viewpoint is quite clear: if you don't work you don't eat. And this is what we must say to many who would become (as some have already become) parasites on our society today because we have encouraged them not to work. Our poverty programs and our welfare programs and all too often our charity programs are designed not to alleviate the problem but to perpetuate the problem, and to encourage people not to work because we will take care of them anyway. I suggest this is immoral and anti-Christian.

Now the justification for this view is as follows:

(1) Pauperizing charity is *harmful to the recipients.* Those who get it are harmed more than they are helped because it destroys their independence, and it destroys the virtues of hard work and honest labor which they could receive by participating. We do it in the name of helping the needy but even such organizations as the Salvation Army, and particularly the Goodwill Industries should have taught us years ago what they learned through experience. They learned that you can help people far more by giving them opportunities to at least in part earn through their efforts and their labors that which we share with them than when we simply make it a "handout" proposition. It destroys the dignity and the independence of the individuals and tends to perpetuate them in that particular status.

(2) It is *harmful to the benefactors.* As far as our government programs are concerned it is a misuse of public funds because it does not eliminate the problem, it intensifies it as I have indicated. And it is certainly a misuse of the Lord's money and charitable funds through our churches and other benevolent enterprises if we are perpetuating the very thing that we are committed to abolish!

(3) It *harms those who are truly needy.* If we are encouraging indolence, laziness, and the lack of acceptance of responsibility on the part of those receiving the handouts from our poverty and welfare programs, and our benevolent and charitable enterprises, then there are *only so many resources available.* If we are misusing and misappropriating these we are denying those who are the victims of their circumstances, particularly the infants, the invalids, and the

elderly which need most desperately our financial assistance.

(4) It is *harmful to society*. It certainly does not encourage industry and initiative to misuse huge sums of tax monies or church gifts for unjustified poverty relieving programs which in effect increase rather than relieve the situation. For instance (if I may oversimplify again) for one businessman to work hard and make a success in his business and then to be so heavily taxed that his neighbor will not have to work at all, but can through the subsistence provided by the industrious neighbor's ability and dedication to his task, live in equitable circumstances, is certainly not an incentive to industry and dedication at his work on the part of the businessman. The misuse of such funds in the name of Christ is certainly a quenching of the spirit of charity and love that ought to be free-flowing from the hearts of God's children. But it has the opposite effect when we see it misused and abused. Rather than intensifying our compassion it quenches it.

The Larger View

Let us not stand behind a facade of conscience-salving cliches in order to eliminate our involvement in alleviating the needs of society. For Paul goes on to say in this very passage (2 Thess. 3:12), "We command and exhort by our Lord Jesus Christ, that with quietness they work, and eat their own bread." He goes on to say to the rest of the church, "But ye, brethren, *be not weary in well-doing*." Now I interpret this to mean that we are to aid the poor. We are to heal the sick. We are to help the indigent. But we are not to encourage laziness and inactivity and overdependence upon others. We are concerned. We are compassionate. But we must not destroy human dignity and responsibility of the individual in sharing from our great abundance.

And a second thing Paul said is, even in exercising church discipline toward those who will not work, you must withdraw from them. He said have no company with them, not for a punitive reason, but *for a remedial purpose.* Discipline in the New Testament is always redemptive and remedial. He says have no company with them in order that they may be ashamed. Help them to see what they are doing that they may be ashamed and repent of it and turn back and become industrious and busy. Verse 15, "Yet count him not as an enemy, but admonish him as a brother." There is no room for hate no matter how indolent a fellow Christian may be, no matter how much of a parasite a man may become, no matter how obnoxious his laziness may appear to our sight. Paul says to withdraw from such a man in the fellowship of the Christian faith so that he may be ashamed, always admonishing as a brother, never treating him as an enemy. There is no room for hatred and bitterness in the Christian's heart.

A final word about motivation needs to be said. An error here would negate the good that otherwise might be accomplished. Everything that is done by the church ministering must be done in Jesus' name, even the giving of a cup of cold water. Service must not be rendered merely to satisfy our "pity glands" but *to help people.* And of course to genuinely help people involves our ministry to their spiritual as well as physical needs. Our task is not, for instance, to Americanize or even to Christianize the world, but to *evangelize* it in obedience to the commands of Christ. We must remember that the church cannot do everything or meet all the personal needs of everybody. Therefore we must do what we do well, and emphasize primarily not what we can do for each other but what God has done for us in Jesus Christ.

XII

NaCl in the Spiritual Realm

NaCl is the chemical formula for sodium chloride or common table salt. It consists of two elements, sodium and chlorine, united together in the proper chemical relationship. Either of these elements alone could be quite harmful to human life, even deadly. Sodium can induce severe and even fatal burns, and chlorine in its very deadly gaseous forms is well known.

Yet these two poisonous substances, when joined together in the right proportions through the proper chemical reaction serve as the basic and complete ingredients for a harmless substance, common table salt! Furthermore such salt is essential to the life, health, and physical well-being of the human body. Such is another phenomenon of human nature and divine creation.

It seems to me that there is an important spiritual analogy to be drawn here also. For this chemical experiment illustrates quite vividly the proper relationship between biblical doctrine and Christian ethics. One cannot exist without the other. Either one taken alone will induce spiritual death. Both are essential to New Testament Christianity and to well-rounded Christian growth and development.

Beliefs and Practices

In other words, it is impossible to agree with those who contend that if your doctrinal beliefs are right, it does not matter how you live. Many Baptists have in a practical way accepted this attitude in their mistaken understanding of the doctrine of eternal security, popularly expressed as "once saved, always saved." The way they live seems to indicate that because of a certain belief they hold, there is no reason to be concerned about godly living.

Of course, this is a complete denial of basic New Testament Christianity, which is always exceedingly practical and relevant to everyday living. It is also a perversion of the biblical doctrine of eternal security of the saints, which doctrine was never intended to be an excuse for loose living. It is a doctrine giving strength and assurance to those struggling Christians who are doing their best to serve God, but are still far short of what they ought to be!

Correct doctrinal beliefs always and inevitably lead to the highest possible ethical conduct! It is simply untrue that one can be correct in doctrinal beliefs if those beliefs are never transformed into practical reality and righteous living. Right belief leads inevitably to right living!

But the obverse is also true. There are those who contend that it doesn't really matter what you believe as long as you *live ethically* and do what is right. Of course this perverted view is poison also to the Christian's life. There can be no right living unless it is built upon and is the outgrowth of right convictions. At least this is true in the highest sense of Christian ethics. It may be that some can live a measure of good conduct without Christian faith, but the highest ethical goodness is achieved only as a result of basic Christian commitment.

Right conduct is based on correct beliefs. Both are essential to the Christian's life, and one cannot be obtained without the other. Just as sodium or chlorine alone would prove detrimental and even deadly to the human body, so trying to be doctrinally sound without godly living, or trying to live right without regard to beliefs and convictions would prove disastrous to the spiritual life. It is the proper combination within the Spirit-filled life of both beliefs and ethics that constitutes a spiritually healthy Christian existence and growth.

Paul's Epistles

A clear example of this interrelatedness between doctrine and ethics may be seen in the epistles of Paul. Often these epistles are outlined under doctrinal and practical divisions. Yet a close reading of these arbitrary outline divisions indicates that the practical section is rich in doctrinal content and the doctrinal section is replete with application, illustration, and practical advice!

Paul never divorced belief and practice. He knew not one without the other. Right Christian conduct was possible only for one who possessed correct Christian beliefs, and Christian doctrine inevitably resulted in righteous living. Look, for example, to Paul's letter to the Galatians. The epistle has been outlined as follows:

I. Personal, chapters 1 and 2
II. Doctrinal, chapters 3 and 4
III. Practical, chapters 5 and 6

Yet notice that in chapter 4, verses 8, 9, and 10 (within the *doctrinal* section) Paul discusses the *practical aspects* of the Galatians' observance of sabbaths, new moons, annual feasts, and years of jubilee. What could be more practical than that? And Paul indicates their practical observance of these events is indicative of their belief!

Again, notice in chapter 5, verses 17 through 25 (within the practical division) Paul teaches many truths about the Holy Spirit, but here particularly as related to the daily Christian life. It is impossible to walk in the Spirit daily, as Paul here teaches, without at least some knowledge of who the Holy Spirit is and what he does—and this is doctrine!

Of course, this is not intended to deny the practical value of arbitrary outline divisions of books of the Bible for analytical purposes! Obviously this is a valuable tool in biblical study. Nevertheless the point is well taken that Paul never conceived of a separation between what the Christian *believed* and the *way he lived!* The first led naturally into the second, which was a natural outgrowth of the first.

Now this is not mere theological hairsplitting. There are few greater needs in this current age than the need to clarify the proper relationship between faith and works, doctrine and ethics, Christian beliefs and Christian conduct. There are varying degrees of emphasis on first one and then the other of these two elements of the Christian revelation, but there must be a concerted effort to bring both into proper relationship and true perspective.

Doctrinal Convictions

It is important that the minister have strong doctrinal convictions, and that he unashamedly bear frequent testimony to these convictions. Unfortunately too many men of the cloth expend their pulpit time in confessing their doubts and illuminating what they do not believe! The trumpets thus sound an uncertain and vitally misleading note. God help us to return to the rudimentary and foundational doctrinal beliefs that have characterized our spiritual forebears and denominational leaders of the past.

Among the doctrinal convictions that must be considered vital for today's ministers of the gospel are the following:

(1) *Belief in God,* as a holy and loving person, a triunity, one who has chosen to make himself known to man whom he has created in his own image. We must believe in *prayer* as a means of communion with God as indicated in Hebrews 11:6. "For he that cometh to God must believe that he is, and that he is a rewarder of them that diligently seek him."

(2) *Belief in man,* as created in the image of God and for fellowship with God. But this image has been marred by man's sin, which is a harsh reality amounting to personal rebellion against God in ungodliness, unrighteousness, and unbelief. Man's only hope to be restored into right relationship with God is through repentance and faith. No person will be saved automatically since God's creation made man a morally responsible human being, who must volitionally come to God for personal redemption.

(3) *Belief in Jesus Christ,* as God's unique Son, essential deity, the God-man, God incarnate, born of a virgin, who gave his life a ransom for many on the cross, who literally died for our sins but rose again for our justification. He is the only way to God, the only hope of salvation, the risen, living, coming again Saviour and Lord. There can be no effective pulpit or personal ministry without an adequate under-

standing of who Jesus is and what God has wrought on our behalf redemptively and spiritually through him!

(4) *Belief in the Bible* as the inspired, authoritative, written Word of God, God-breathed and Spirit-directed, our only rule of faith and practice. The great need of this generation of preachers is for more Bible study in depth resulting in more frequent exposition of Scripture from the pulpit! We are faced with a generation of Bible-ignorant worshipers who desperately need a fresh word from the old Book. It is time to do more than just defend our faith in the Bible as God's Word; *we must preach the Bible as God's Word to modern man!*

The Practical Side

But there must also be the practical side of such strong doctrinal beliefs (as we have seen). And this practical aspect involves additional doctrinal convictions. Someone has well said the minister must believe in the *holy life*, the *Holy Spirit*, and the *Holy Book*. The preacher must be a man of moral purity and spiritual devotion. If he is not committed unreservedly to godly living, he cannot possibly lead his people in that direction.

Yet he must realize that there is no victorious daily living apart from a personal, workable acquaintance with the person of the Holy Spirit. Also the minister must not neglect the reading of the Scriptures as a source of personal guidance and inspiration for himself. Too frequently we read the Bible only in searching for a text, while neglecting our personal needs for daily feeding our own souls.

The Holy Spirit is a person, and he is also God. Correct practical application of this biblical doctrine in the daily life of the Christian is a classic example of the necessity for a healthy sodium chloride type balance between doctrine and ethics. One would not know how to begin to live the Christian life if he did not have *some* knowledge of the person and work of the Holy Spirit, who is the Spirit of Christ and of God.

Reference has been made in a previous chapter to the necessity of the church breaking out of its exclusive shell and literally going into the world for ministry and service. This is a part of the works side of the gospel. It is insufficient to "believe only" if our faith does not find its fruition in active, good works. As James said, "Faith without works is dead."

It is important in applying this two-pronged fork of Christian faith and works to avoid the pitfall of playing God or assuming the role of the Holy Spirit for another person. This is a particular danger for the minister or counselor. It is all too easy to usurp the divine prerogatives and pronounce judgment upon another person's faith and/or works. But the minister's role is always that of *adviser* and *undershepherd,* rather than judge and jury. We must attempt to adequately present both aspects of the Christian revelation in clear and understandable terms, but who are we to issue final directives as to where the emphasis ought to be placed in a given individual's life?

In conclusion, we as ministers need to be conscious of the delicate balance between faith and works in our own lives, ministries, and preaching, but resist succumbing to the ever present temptation to become judgmental and vindictive, rather than loving. There is need for strong, doctrinal convictions and the preaching of these to today's congregations. But there is equally a great need for relevant application of the practical aspects of the gospel implications. We cannot afford the luxury of indifference to doctrine and truth on the one hand, *or* the practical neglect of applied Christianity to the issues of the day on the other. Trite it may well be, but true it definitely is to say that it is not either/or but both/and.

There has appeared, unfortunately, in recent years an unholy dichotomy between faith and works, between individual personal redemption and ethical responsibility. This is an unfortunate polarization and a nonbiblical absolutizing of complementary, scriptural truths. Jesus was obviously interested in man's physical problems, including hunger, disease, bereavement, mental derangement, and personal economics. But Jesus resisted the temptation to minister exclusively to physical needs, which would have reduced man to the level of the animals. Jesus knew (more than any of us) that man is *more than a physical being;* that he is *inherently a spiritual being* created for personal fellowship with God. Only by accurately recognizing this twofold, universal need of mankind can the minister of today adequately maintain the delicate but necessary balance between correct beliefs and godly living.

XIII

The Old Green-Eyed Monster

Perhaps every profession and occupation has its own special problem, its peculiar "monster" that plagues practically every person involved within its particular activities. There are, no doubt, problems exclusively or at least especially related to certain areas of work. Many jobs contain built-in dangers and temptations.

The ministry is certainly no exception! There are, of course, many pitfalls and stumbling stones in the path of the man of the cloth. Problems for some would not necessarily be applicable to all. There are certainly many common temptations, however, as we have seen. But it seems apparent to me that there is one grand bugaboo that plagues practically the entire ministry as a profession (or calling). I refer to the old green-eyed monster, *envy*, or its deadly offspring, *jealousy*.

The *Thorndike-Barnhart Junior Dictionary* graphically defines these two synonyms as follows: *Envy* is discontent or ill will at another's good fortune because one wishes it had been his; dislike for a person who has what one wants. *Jealousy* is described as feeling as a person does when people who usually pay attention to him neglect him and pay much attention to somebody else. (Webster defines *green-eyed* as seeing with jealous eyes; biased by jealousy.)

Does this sound like the way preachers often feel towards each other? Listen again: Discontent at another's good fortune because one wishes it had been his, and the feeling of neglect when much attention is paid someone else! Surely this is a sad commentary on many actual ministerial attitudes today. All too frequently the fellowship and rapport between ministers of the gospel is marred or rendered impossible because of the ever present green-eyed monster!

Yet, of all people, ministers should be the ones to get along admirably. They should manifest true brotherly kindness above all others. Theirs ought to be the closest of interpersonal relationships within common professions, fraternities, business enterprises, or callings. But, alas, the opposite is too frequently true. Where there should be respect and admiration, where there should be Christian love and affection, there is occasionally and sometimes perennially, jealousy and envy.

This two-headed, green-eyed monster is the enemy of the soul, the cancer of the spiritual bloodstream, the ugly canker on the spiritual life. It is poisonous, insipid, rotten, and finally, fatal to one's influence and effectiveness as a minister of the gospel. There is no justification for its presence, yet its reality is apparent and its shuddering results are available for all to see. Wherever it raises its ugly head the progress of the gospel is thwarted and the church of Christ is placed in ill repute. Let some noble soldier of the cross go forward and slay this mighty dragon, lest the ministry destroy itself in the venom of its own maladjustments and emotional immaturity!

Necessity for Interdependence

No other occupation, however, inherently demands such absolute interdependence for survival as does the ministry. We are dependent upon one another to a unique degree. "None of us liveth to himself, and no man dieth to himself" (Rom. 14:7) was never more true than in relation to preachers! The greatest friend a preacher could have ought to be another preacher! We ought to pray for one another, love one another, and rejoice in one another's successes and accomplishments. It is high time we grew up into enough Christian maturity to be able to at least partially demonstrate to the church and the world what New Testament *koinonia* is all about!

Let me quote again John 13:35, where Jesus, himself, said, "By this shall all men know that ye are my disciples, *if ye have love one to another.*" Then listen to the words of 1 John 3:14-16, "We know that we have passed from death unto life, because we love the brethren. He that loveth not his brother abideth in death. Whosoever hateth his brother is a murderer: and ye know that no murderer hath eternal life abiding in him. Hereby perceive we the love of God, because he laid down his life for us: and we ought to lay down our lives for the brethren."

Strange words indeed are these in all too many ministerial circles today! Let us not be falsely pious, brethren, and deny the reality we all know exists. What about character assassination, malicious spreading of immoral tales (whether true or not, it matters not), and vicious undercutting of another's rapport with his own people? We all stand condemned, I am afraid, before the searchlight of divine omniscience. Let us bow down before the God of all mercies and confess our faults, first to him and then to each other, for our hands are also full of blood—the blood that should be the tie that binds our hearts in Christian love with those fellow pilgrims who are our co-laborers in the Lord.

Confess One to Another

James said, "Confess your faults one to another, and pray one for another, that ye may be healed" (5:16). Brethren, that is the only cure for the green-eyed monster! Although some sins are by their very nature personal and private, and therefore need only to be confessed to God, the sins of jealousy and envy need to be acknowledged openly, at least as far as the object of jealousy and envy is concerned. How, for instance, could we ever truly purge our souls of this deadly evil if we never acknowledged our guilt and repentance to the one whose glory and success precipitated our default? Confess one to another, brethren; it is good therapy for the soul!

Recently a fellow minister, whom I had always held in highest esteem, came to me with a deep conviction of the necessity for confessing his feelings of envy toward me, my church, and my ministry. It was initially an embarrassing moment for me, as it was a difficult one for him. I could not at first see the need of such a confession anyway. I had been unaware of any such feelings on his part. He was my friend! Yet he felt the need of ridding his soul of that just born but rapidly growing green-eyed monster, and he slew it in one fell swoop, with an honest confession to God and to his brother in Christ. My respect and affection for this friend has only been intensified. I hope and pray that I shall be as honest and forthright when the circumstance is reversed!

Yet I can recall the occasion when I was the instigator of ill will and tense, strained emotions. It took some praying and some personal soul searching, but I had no relief until the offended minister was sought out personally and privately, and I confessed openly to him my remorse, regret, and repentance. My only afterthought was simply as to why it took so long to return to fundamental Christian principles, especially for a minister of the gospel!

Relationships to Former Pastors

One of the most frequent areas of occurrence of this problem in ministerial relationships is in regard to former pastors returning to the church field. Of course, I have heard all my ministry that this practice is unethical, it should not be done, and many problems are created as a result of it. And no doubt there *have been* many difficult situations created as a result of unethical ministerial practices in regard to former pastorates.

Yet I must testify to a most delightful total experience in regard to this matter. In the first place, I recall with joy the warm attitude and friendliness of the immediate successor to my first pastorate. In fact his friendship and genuine interest resulted in my family and me moving our church membership back to this former pastorate during a period when I was in evangelism. This was a blessed relationship, and not just one-sided, as evidenced in the fact the church voted unanimously to pay the evangelist's expenses to the Southern Baptist Convention.

My attitude toward my predecessors has consciously been built upon this memorable relationship. I can honestly say that *all* of my predecessors are *genuinely welcome to come back home* whenever their own pressing schedules allow. In fact several of these men have become some of the best friends I have on earth. Thus their counsel and advice (solicited by me) has been, in some instances, of great value.

Actually what does the pastor stand to lose by being friendly and demonstrating Christian courtesy to his predecessors? Not one thing, in my opinion. Actually those people who were enraptured in someone else's ministry will appreciate the present pastor even more for his graciousness in inviting the former pastor back to visit. How much better it is for an *occasion* to be made with aforethought and dignity, than for a former pastor to feel the necessity of creeping in unawares, so to speak. No congregation will think less of its pastor for his magnanimous spirit and genuine Christian friendship with other ministers.

It is possible to propagate an unconscious attitude of envy through traditional and ill-advised concepts of so-called ministerial ethics. We can hide behind this cliche to the point of nausea. It is time to challenge some of these ridiculous interpretations of ministerial ethics and reveal them unmasked for what they really often are, namely, unmitigated ministerial jealousy.

Why should there be such a feeling within the ministry that one must constantly be on guard against his fellow ministers? We had best learn to stay together and pray together, or we shall soon hang separately as has been suggested. A good rule of thumb in ministerial ethics, it seems to me, is simply to apply the Golden Rule! Isn't that amazing? We need to act and react toward our fellow ministers like Jesus taught Christians to act all the time anyway. My, what a revolution in ministerial circles would be precipitated if we preachers would just start acting like Christians toward one another.

Denominational Politics

A great contributor toward the ascendancy of the green-eyed monster is that very real but unspoken demon, denominational politics. I love my denomination. It has contributed greatly to my ministry and to my personal life. But unfortunately just like the local church, it consists of leaders and workers who are all too human and frail. Thus a well meaning and justifiable, even essential organization, can become an instrument of divisiveness, pettiness, and false pride. An otherwise efficient and altruistic person can became an old crab or a possessive, demanding octopus almost overnight, if he gets bitten by the bug of denominational politics!

Perhaps we need to return to a sense of basic values in dealing with this disturbing situation. The most important, the most significant, and the most honorable position a Baptist preacher can occupy is not the presidency of the Convention or some other high denominational office. It is *to be the pastor of a local Baptist church!* This is the top position and the greatest honor. Let us not forget that, and let us conduct our denominational affairs accordingly.

The greatest friends I have in the world are preachers. I thank God for them, and I pray that God will remove any spark of envy or jealousy within my heart and life that may be there. We need to deepen our partnership, not split it. We need to increase our fellowship, not suppress it. We need to practice our belief in brotherly love, not eradicate it. The world awaits a candid demonstration of true Christian agape, and its eyes are focused upon the church and its leaders who call themselves preachers of the gospel. Where are the living epistles?

XIV

Integrity—The Need of the Hour

In the midst of all the problems and conflicts in our confused world of today the greatest need is that of personal integrity on the part of the minister himself. By this is meant genuine Christian character, the real self being sterling, genuine, and pure! Without this nothing else will help. With this there is a foundation upon which a successful ministry can be built.

The minister, like the poet, must realize the imperative necessity of implementing that well-known phrase, "To thine own self be true." The pastor can deceive his people, his family, even himself, but not forever. It is essential that he of all people be able to see himself clearly as he faces the mirror each day.

A preacher in the New Testament was a proclaimer, a *kerux*. In the Christian context this means he was a public disseminator of the good news about Jesus Christ. He was called of God and impowered by the Spirit to preach redemption through Christ. The minister is thus to be a God-called, Christ-redeemed, Spirit-regenerated man whose supreme purpose in life is to manifest through his life and ministry the person and work of Jesus Christ. This high, lofty concept, of course, is an indictment of me and all preachers. It is not easy to be that kind of man of God. All of us fall far short. Yet this must be our constant goal, aim, and aspiration. Each man must have a burning desire in his heart to be the ideal, the Christ-centered preacher, a man of unquestionable integrity.

Integrity in the life of the minister must, of course, be applied to every area. This includes the pulpit, public or community relationships, the minister's home and family life, as well as his social, economic, and denominational responsibilities. The validity of the gospel message is not dependent upon the minister's personal integrity, thank God! The gospel is validated by the integrity of Jesus Christ. However, the *effectiveness* of the gospel witness is impaired by lack of integrity in the minister's makeup in whatever area it might reveal itself.

Three Descriptive Words

Now the minister of the gospel, if he is a man of integrity and has truly committed himself to Jesus Christ and his understanding of the divine call, can be characterized by at least these three descriptive words: security, serenity, and spirituality. First, the minister's *security* is not to be found in outward circumstances, financial income, attitudes of church members or deacons, or community situations. His security is found in the God who called him to preach, the Christ who redeemed him and to whom he has committed his life! The insecurity of many ministers today is directly related to a basic fallacy on the minister's part. If we put our faith and confidence in human beings or physical and material things, we cannot help but develop insecurity, since these things will pass away. The insecurity of many ministers today is readily identifiable because of the transitoriness of so much that is visible in the world of the twentieth century. Preoccupation with material things is the blight of our modern world, and ministers are infected also. Once again preachers of today must be called back to a basic premise of Christian faith, namely, our security is in the Lord Christ and not in outward circumstances and situations.

Second, the minister must be *serene.* He must maintain inner peace in the midst of outward adversity. His is the peace that truly passes human understanding. He is the epitomy of a calm within a storm. He demonstrates what he preaches and becomes the comforter, the man of God in a time of crisis. If the minister reacts emotionally and irrationally at the slightest provocation, his people will follow suit. Their spiritual growth will in all probability never surpass that of their spiritual leader. Confidence is instigated in the hearts of people whose spiritual leader manifests a confident serenity based upon deep, spiritual devotion.

Third, the minister must be above all a deeply *spiritual* man. Of course I do not mean by this a syrupy sentimentality, an effected piousity, or the frequent repetition of pious platitudes. Spirituality is not a pious manner, but it is primarily a matter of the performance of the will of God, obedience to Jesus Christ, and living under the leadership and direction of the Holy Spirit. Spirituality means following the Holy Spirit's leadership. A spiritual man is a real man, not a sissy, nor a coward.

This is the kind of dynamic leadership the world and our churches stand so desperately in need of today—ministers who are secure in Christ, serene within their own hearts, and led by the Spirit of God. These are the men who demonstrate integrity in every human and divine relationship. Occasionally parents tell their children, "You better be on your best behavior, the preacher is coming!" Or even after the minister arrives, "The preacher is here, you had better be good!" Yet Jesus is here all the time. If a child is taught only to be good while the preacher is present, he will not have inner spiritual resources sufficient for those moments of temptation that are sure to come. If we are taught to be good only in church or while someone is looking, then we as ministers of the gospel are sure to fail in the times of acid testing. It is true for preachers as well as for others. Remember, the Lord is at hand!

The Heart of the Matter

The Christian faith is all about the heart, motives, inner thoughts, and feelings. Integrity is essential for true Christianity. Ministers often insist that there is no double standard. We loudly proclaim that people have put us on a pedestal, set us on a high tower, that we live in a goldfish bowl and people condemn in us what they excuse in themselves. No matter how true this may be, the minister needs to realize this is a two-edged sword which works both ways. We have no right to preach one standard of morals and ethics and live another! We must practice in the innermost recesses of our beings what we preach and expect our people to follow.

It has been said that the real test of a man's integrity is what he would do in a given instance if he knew no one would ever find out. But for the Christian and especially the minister of the gospel this does not hold true. In the first place in the act of committing sin *someone* has already found *out!* God knows it and even more significant perhaps, the individual knows it. Sin contains the seeds of its own judgment. And although no one else may ever find out, the character of the individual committing the act of wilful rebellion and sin is drastically affected. The wrath of God in operation means simply that such a person is being given over to his sins as he persists in choosing them. To persist in sin is inevitably to be given up to sin, resulting in a reprobate mind devoid of spiritual discernment.

In this day and age it is possible for the minister to fly many, many miles away from his church field, where he will be unknown, where he might succumb to the temptations precipitated by distance, anonymity, and unfamiliarity. But the rushing judgment for sin and the experience that at least in part is in the initial commitment of sin cannot be escaped. No minister can maintain the purity of heart essential for being an effective medium for the propagation of the gospel who sacrifices his integrity on the altar of indulgence under the guise of anonymity.

What the Minister Can Do

Actually there are four things a minister can do to help maintain his personal integrity and spirituality. These are:

(1) *Walk* in the Spirit. The Scripture teaches us that victory in Christ in daily living is *not in the will but in the walk.* It is not enough to merely *want* to do right or decide to do it, we must have supernatural assistance. The Scripture says, "Wherefore let him that thinketh he standeth take heed lest he fall" (1 Cor. 10:12). Every time a fellow minister falls morally, each of us in the eyes of the people fall just a little bit with him. But each instance can also be an opportunity for a recommitment of our lives to Jesus Christ, realizing that every Christian and every minister is capable of committing

any sin in the book. The only alternative is a persistent daily walk in the Spirit of Christ.

(2) *Reckon.* Paul indicates in Romans 6 that we are to reckon ourselves to be dead indeed unto sin but alive unto God. To reckon it to be so is to act like it is true, to live like it. The minister indeed is crucified with Christ yet he goes on living, susceptible to the same temptations, lusts of the flesh, and other things. The only possible way to escape the downfall that sometimes seems so imminent is to account or reckon oneself to be dead unto sin, but alive unto God through Jesus Christ. The Christian is a dead man, who has died with Christ, but has been raised again to newness of life.

(3) Then there is the call to *obey.* Jesus said, "Why call ye me Lord, Lord, and do not the things which I say?" Saul had a rational explanation for not slaying all of the animals contrary to divine direction. His reply to Samuel's inquiry was that he intended to use the animals for sacrifice to Jehovah. Samuel's reply was, "To obey is better than sacrifice, and to hearken than the fat of rams." All of our rational explanations, all references to extenuating circumstances, all personal excuses and justifications for failure are not worth as much in God's sight as simple obedience to his specific commands. To do the will of God is always paramount.

(4) Finally there is the need to *pray.* This is one of the most neglected functions in the minister's routine. It is far easier to preach on prayer and to talk about it, to quote Scriptures, to search for cross references, and so forth, than to pray. The most difficult task the minister has is that which ought to be the most essential, namely, talking with God. Of all the definitions this is by far the best: Prayer is *talking with God.*

Although prayer may involve thanksgiving, praise, worship, petition, confessions, intercession, and all the rest, it is essentially communion with God. Such communion is impossible unless the minister is a man of integrity. We can be hypocritical in everything except worship and prayer. There is no pretension before God. We might pretend publicly, but real prayer is possible only through intimate, personal communion with the Heavenly Father. The minister must work hard at cultivating prayer, a meaningful devotional life, and other spiritual activities for the soul.

A Real Man of God

It is a great thrill to be a minister of the gospel. It is an awesome responsibility, but it is the highest calling and I am glad to be a preacher. I can still hear the trumpets in the morning. It is my prayer that someone whose spiritual hearing has been dulled will as a result of this personal spiritual pilgrimage be able to once again hear the sound, answer the call, and stand up to be a *real man of God.*

The epistle of 2 Timothy is actually an exhortation for the minister of the gospel to be a real man of God. Many and varied are the qualifications for the man of God, but at least these four outstanding challenges are evident in this epistle.

The real man of God must be a *man of the Spirit.* "Wherefore I put thee in remembrance that thou stir up the gift of God, which is in thee by the putting on of my hands. For God hath not given us the spirit of fear; but of power, and of love, and of a sound mind" (1:6-7). Timothy had evidently received a special gift of the Spirit at the time of his ordination to the gospel ministry at the hands of the apostle Paul. He is exhorted to stir up this gift, or literally to again bring fire to the life, the two words in English "stir up" being a translation of one word which is a combination of three words meaning *again, life,* and *fire.*

God is not the author of timidity, fearfulness, and anxiety, the apostle reminds Timothy and all ministers. God is rather the author of *dunamis, agape,* and a *healthy mind.* What a relevant message for ministers of this day and age! It is almost as if Paul were writing today rather than two thousand years ago. Such is the glorious mystery of inspiration in God's written Word.

Of course, Paul reminds Timothy in verse 14, "That good thing which was committed unto thee keep by the Holy Ghost which dwelleth in us." The only way to keep that which has been committed unto us as ministers of the gospel is by the Holy Spirit. If integrity is the need of the hour (and it is) then we must depend upon the Holy Spirit to maintain our integrity, not upon our own will power or strength of conviction.

The real man of God must also be a man *of strong determination* and conviction. In 2 Timothy 2:1, Paul challenged Timothy to *be strong* in the grace that is in Christ Jesus. In verse 15 he exhorts the young minister to *be studious* or diligent as an unashamed workman affirmed of God. In verse 22 Paul indicates the real man of God must be *sterling in character.* "Flee also youthful lusts: but follow righteousness, faith, charity, peace, with them that call on the Lord out of a pure heart." This entire epistle seems dedicated to the proposition that integrity is the basic need of the hour!

Additionally the minister should be *a man of the Scriptures* (3:14-17). "But continue thou in the things which thou hast learned and hast been assured of, knowing of whom thou hast learned them; and that from a child thou hast known the holy scriptures, which are able to make thee wise unto salvation through faith which is in Christ Jesus. All scripture is given by inspiration of God, and is profitable for doctrine, for reproof, for correction, for instruction in righteousness; that the man of God may be perfect, thoroughly furnished unto all good works." There is no substitute for basic knowledge of the Scriptures for today's ministry. No amount of secular knowledge, knowledge of poetry, drama, history, and literature can ever take the place of knowing the holy Scriptures. The main resource for the preacher has always been and will ever be the Scriptures. God himself is the source of all Scripture, and the preacher's principle resource is the Scriptures.

But the minister of integrity must also be a *man of sound doctrine* (4:1-5). Paul warned of false doctrine and indicated the answer to false doctrine is to preach the Word at all times and watch in all things. The word "sound" means healthy, and the minister's spiritual health, as well as that of his people, is to a great degree dependent upon the exposition of sound, healthy doctrine.

Thus the epistle of 2 Timothy has been outlined broadly as indicating the characteristics of the minister of genuineness and integrity. He is to be a man of the Spirit (chapter 1), a man of strong conviction (chapter 2), a man of the Book (chapter 3), and a man of sound doctrine (chapter 4). God help us to be real ministers of the gospel and men of integrity! Only thus can we properly respond to the trumpets in the morning!